Jesus Loves Me

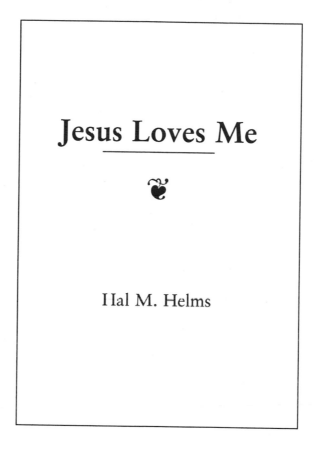

Jesus Loves Me

Hal M. Helms

PARACLETE PRESS
BREWSTER, MASSACHUSETTS

Library of Congress Cataloging-in-Publication Data

Helms, Hal McElwaine.
    Jesus loves me / Hal M. Helms.
        p. cm.
    ISBN 1-55725-185-1 (pbk.)
    1. Catholic Church—Prayer—books and devotions—English. 2. Devotional calendars.   I. Title.
    BX2110.H45   1997
    242'.2—dc21
                                                96-52307
                                                CIP

10 9 8 7 6 5 4 3 2 1

© 1996 Paraclete Press
ISBN #: 1-55725-185-1

Published by Paraclete Press,
Brewster, Massachusetts
Printed in the United States of America

Week One

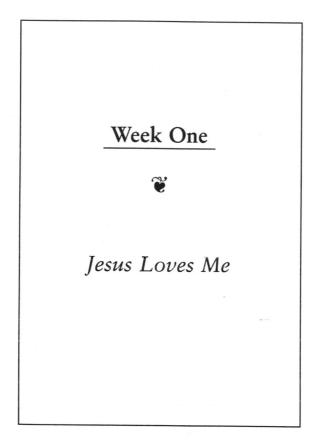

Jesus Loves Me

Jesus Loves Me, This I Know . . .

We all remember this familiar hymn as a comforting reminder of God's love—but do we *really* believe it? Are we convinced that God loves us *no matter what*? And how do we receive this message? Despite what the media says, love is not free - although it is freely given. Love cost our Lord *everything*. What is it worth to us?

We begin this first week looking at God's amazing and unconditional love! He loves us "with an everlasting love", and the Bible gives proof after proof of His faithfulness. We oftentimes have flawed concepts and images of God floating in our minds—perhaps a stern old man with a beard, ready to punish at a moment's notice. Yet the truth is that God is gentle, and He loves us perfectly—not in spite of who we are, but *because* of who we are: His sons and daughters! Do we really believe that? Can we really trust that? Yes we can!

"Jesus loves me, this I know, for the Bible tells me so . . . !"

This I Know

Scripture: John 3:16-21

*Text: God so loved the world that He gave
His only Son. . . .   (John 3:16)*

Today we begin a new cycle of devotional exercises. It can be an exciting, growing time if we will allow the Holy Spirit to teach us and guide us in these weeks ahead. There is for every one of us a great deal of "unexplored territory" in our walk with the Lord. So let us pray together that the Blessed Spirit will be our companion, fulfilling the promise of Jesus: "He will bear witness to me." (John 15:26)

We begin with one of the most familiar hymns and probably the most familiar text in the entire Bible:

Jesus loves me, this I know,
For the Bible tells me so.

"God so loved *the world* that He gave His only Son, that whoever believes in Him should not perish but have eternal life."

This is the Gospel in a nutshell—the Good News that should bring joy and gladness to everyone who hears it. But don't we have difficulty believing it to be true? Don't we easily say words that do not penetrate the depth of the heart and make a difference in the way we face life? I think we do.

First, we need to hear what love cost God. This is not a cheap bit of good will to naughty children. This is a love that reaches so far, so wide, and so deep that it struggles with all the darkness that destroys the peace and harmony of the world. It is a love that dares to confront the wickedness that wastes human lives on many levels—the wickedness that sets itself against God's laws; the iniquity that closes the heart to

4

the rays of light that God sends it; the evil that would build a kingdom in which God has no part, a kingdom of perversity and death.

We live in a time when the forces of darkness are very bold. They have unmasked themselves in many ways, and challenge anyone who dares oppose them. We need not mention all of them, but any sober-minded person can see that there is a powerful effort to turn upside down the standards of morality and of right and wrong.

Jesus loves me? Does it matter how I try to live in this strange and increasingly estranged world? It matters more than we realize, and it matters more and more.

A great battle has been waged, and the enemy lost it. It was waged by a lone figure who walked on the stage of history and died a shameful death on a cross. It was waged when the sun hid its face and darkness descended at noon. It was won by losing. A Life was given up so that life could reign against the cult of death. That battle was won, and Jesus invites us to share in its victory. His love lures us into costly choices: choosing life instead of death; choosing to learn what it means to love Him in return for His love.

Yes, Jesus loves me . . . and you . . . and you . . . and you.

Prayer: My Jesus, I love Thee, I know Thou art mine. For Thee all the follies of sin I resign. My gracious Redeemer, my Savior art Thou: if ever I loved Thee, my Jesus, 'tis now.

(A. J. Gordon)

1. What was the cost to God of his love for us?

2. Against what do you have to struggle when you seek to follow Jesus and respond to his love?

The Resurrection and the Life

Scripture: I John 4:7-11

Text: Beloved, let us love one another, for love is of
God . . . ; for God is love.   (I John 4:7a and 8b)

"Yes, Jesus loves me; the Bible tells me so." And so it does—
His love glows on every page. The Bible has been called
"God's love-letter to the world."

People have all kinds of ideas about what God is like.
Children picture Him as an old man with a long beard—perhaps
confusing Him with pictures of Father Time or Moses! I'm
not sure they shed all these images when they grow up.

A lot of people, including Christians, view God as a stern
lawgiver, waiting to mark up iniquities and sins, and ready to
punish when we fail to live up to His decrees. Many people
never really shed this negative view of God, and whole books
have been written contrasting the God of the Old Testament
(Lawgiver) with the God of the New Testament (God of
Mercy). Yet Jesus taught us to call God "Our Father."

If we are going to make progress in our walk with God, we
must correct the mistaken images we have carried in our
hearts. We must begin to take seriously what God says about
Himself, and today's text is about as clear as we could ever
hope to find. "God is love."

The Christian life is a life of discovery. It is a life of learning who God is by living and walking with Him. We come to
Him with a lot of confused ideas and concepts. That is to be
expected and is not something to worry about. But then we
begin to learn "who He is," not by reading a lot of books on
theology, but by living. Every day is a schoolday of faith. We
are being taught as we are being led. He is correcting our

6

faulty ideas and fantasies by the way He deals with us. And that is a sure way of ending our journey with a clearer vision of God than we began.

Yes, God does hold up certain standards of thought and life for us. These are life-standards, meant to provide a framework in which the inner life can grow. They include honesty, decency, faithfulness in keeping our word, truthfulness in speech, reverence towards our Creator, and respect for one another. But they are not "traps" to catch us and punish us. They are conditions that enable the love-relationship to grow.

But we do not keep those standards, and we all fall short of them. What then? Are we consigned to the dust-heap of history? On the contrary, we become the objects of a love-search on the part of God who is love. His love will not let us go, and we will learn that He can be a persistent Searcher of souls.

Prayer: The journey has begun, Father, and our hearts would learn the lessons fit for the day. Teach us what we most need to know, and speak the word we most need to hear; we ask in Jesus' name. Amen.

1. How has God's love been demonstrated to you through the circumstances and events of your life?

2. Why do we need the framework of God's standards of thought and life?

How Can It Be?

Scripture: Ephesians 2:1-10

*Text: For by grace you have been saved through faith;
and this is not your own doing, it is the gift of God—
not because of works. . . .   (Ephesians 2:8, 9a)*

It was Charles Wesley who wrote these words: "And can it be that I should gain an interest in the Savior's blood? Died He for me, who caused His pain? For me, who Him to death pursued? Amazing love! How can it be that Thou, my Lord, should'st die for me?"

Someone said recently that our Christian life is like a spiral. It begins in love, and love leads to self-knowledge. Self-knowledge leads us to penitence and penitence brings forgiveness, which brings us back to love. An ascending, but never-ending spiral as we are confronted at deeper levels with the wonder of God's amazing love.

There is an amusing story of an old lady who remarked after hearing a very moving sermon on the love of God. "Well," she said, "If Jesus Christ does save me, He'll never hear the end of it!" Maybe that's what our Christian life should be all about: making sure that He never hears the end of our wonder and gratitude for all He has done.

Our hearts easily grow callous, however. When we allow the self-righteous side of our natures to prevail, we may become convinced that we are not so bad—"certainly not as bad as *those* people who break all the rules and seem to get away with it"—and so we can easily lose touch with the wonder of His love. This is why we need to come against that within us that would put a barrier between us and our Savior. This is why we need to listen when someone—anyone—tells us "bad news" about ourselves. Our instinct may be to reject whatever they are saying or implying about our fault—but if we do, we are the losers, for we purchase that bit of self-justification at a great price: the hardening of our hearts against our Savior.

In many traditions, the worship service begins with the words "Kyrie eleison," "Lord, have mercy." Why? Because the whole company of people is expressing a great need. When we come before the Majesty on high, when we stand before our Creator, like Isaiah we become aware that we are a people of unclean lips, thoughts, and deeds. (Isaiah 6) His light and glory reveal our own stains and smudges, and we *know* that we need His mercy. When we have been welcomed and assured of His gracious disposition toward us, then, and only then, can we relax in His presence. George Herbert said:

> Love bade me welcome; yet my soul drew back,
>   Guilty of dust and sin,
> But quick-eyed Love, observing me grow slack
>   From my first entrance in,
> Drew nearer to me, sweetly questioning,
>   If I lacked anything.

Such is the wonder of His love. "How can it be?" Only because of who He is, because our God so loved us that He determined to woo and win us to life!

Prayer: "'Tis mercy all! let earth adore; Let angel minds inquire no more."

(Wesley)

1. According to this passage in Ephesians, what is the end result of our natural desires and thoughts?

2. How has God intervened in the process, and with what result?

9

Standing on God's Promises

Scripture: II Peter 1:1-4

Text: ". . . He has granted to us His precious and very great promises, that through these you may escape from the corruption that is in the world because of passion, and become partakers of the divine nature." (II Peter 1:4)

"Standing on the promises of God my Savior, standing on the promises of God." Millions of people have sung those words, and perhaps we have sung them many times, carried away with the catchy, bouncy tune and hardly grasping the import of what we are saying.

A promise is no better than the one who makes it. I'm afraid that all of us have made promises and failed to keep them. If that becomes an established pattern, we lose our credibility and people pay no attention. A few generations ago many men took a lot of pride in keeping their word. "A man's word is his bond," they said. And if a person was known to be "a person of his word," he was highly esteemed by the whole community. If, on the other hand, he was known as a man of easy speech, people would avoid any serious business with Him if they could.

God is very careful to back up His promise with His own character. In one place the Bible says, "Since He had no one greater by whom to swear, He swore by Himself, saying, 'Surely I will bless you and multiply you.'" (Heb. 6:13) Having put His own character and, as it were, His own reputation on the line, He is very careful in fulfilling what He has promised. Thus we see in Jesus' life a cataloging of the promises that came in many ways in the history of God's people.

What God did in Jesus was to fulfill every good promise

that He had made since the days of Adam and Eve. "All the promises of God find their yes and amen in Him," says Paul. When we look into the life of Jesus, we do not simply see a man who suddenly appears and follows obediently what He is shown as the Father's will. We see more than that. We see the One who was to come, the embodiment of God's gracious will towards all who shall come to love Him.

"And he [Joseph] went and dwelt in a city called Nazareth, *that what was spoken by the prophets might be fulfilled*, 'He shall be called a Nazarene.'" (Matthew 2:23)

"*This was done to fulfill what was spoken by the prophet Isaiah*: 'Behold, my servant whom I have chosen, my beloved with whom my soul is well pleased.'" (Matthew 12:17)

And finally, Jesus said when He was arrested: "But how then should the Scriptures be fulfilled, that it must be so?" (Matthew 26:54).

So it is right and proper to say, when we place our trust in Jesus, "I am standing on the promises of God!" For so we are.

Prayer: For all Your precious and very great promises, we thank You, blessed Lord. For their perfect fulfillment in Jesus our Savior. May we ever stand sure, knowing that You always fulfill Your word. Amen.

1. According to this passage, what has been given to us through the knowledge of God and Jesus?

2. What do God's promises enable us to do?

When Doubt and Fears Assail

Scripture: Matthew 7:24-27

Text: . . . But it did not fall, because it had been founded on the rock.   (Matthew 7:25)

Thinking again of that old Gospel song, "Standing on the Promises," the words continue this way: "Standing on the promises I cannot fail, when the howling storms of doubt and fear assail; by the living Word of God I shall prevail, Standing on the promises of God."

The Bible has much to say about foundations and the importance of them. This parable of Jesus which we read today sums up His concern that we build on a dependable foundation. It seems from the story that the houses were very much alike. There is no indication that one was a well-built house and the other a poor one. The difference was the foundation on which they were set.

Every child of God experiences "the howling storms of doubt and fear" at times. We are subject to self-doubt as well as to the assaults of the enemy of our souls. The annals of faith, the record of people who have loved God and lived for Him, are filled with the confession that even the bravest souls are sometimes "almost overcome" with these dark, faithless thoughts. In *Pilgrim's Progress*, Christian and Hopeful found themselves in the hands of Giant Despair, who threw them into the Doubting Castle. By this the author shows us that doubts and fears are very likely to be our lot in this journey.

What are we to do when we are under such attack of thought and feeling? When we do not feel loved or sure of our relationship with God? We are to "stand therefore," as Paul said, and, "having done all, to stand." Learning to doubt our doubts, learning to practice thanksgiving even when we do not *feel* thankful, learning to praise God even when we have no conscious assurance of His love—these are weapons in our warfare. They are sure answers to the corrosive work of the enemy of souls. Doubt and fear are his best weapons, to undermine our life's faith and work.

There is an old spiritual which says, "I shall not be moved!" Sometimes we cannot make the progress we would like. For various reasons, we have halted in our spiritual progress. But we *can* by the grace of God say, "I shall not be moved." That sure foundation on which we placed our "house of faith" is none other than Jesus Christ, our Redeemer and Savior. He has purchased us with the price of His own life, and has called us His own. That is the truth, and in spite of the clouds that may cover the sky on any particular day, the truth stands.

Yes, Jesus loves *you*. Stand on His promises.

Prayer: In all the turmoil and uncertainty of life, Father, keep us steadfast, planted on the sure Rock of Your faithfulness; through Jesus Christ our Lord. Amen.

1. The wise man and the foolish man both heard the words of Jesus. What was the difference between them?

2. What do the raging winds, and flooding streams represent in your life?

Light on the Path

Scripture: II Peter 1:12-21; Ephesians 5:11-14

*Text: You will do well to pay attention to this as to a lamp
shining in a dark place. . . . (II Peter 1:19)*

*You once were darkness, but now you are light in the Lord;
walk as children of light. . . . (Ephesians 5:8)*

There are many dark places in this walk of faith. There are
many situations in which we cannot easily or immediately
see all we would like to see. There are many mysteries that
will not be solved in this earthly life of ours. Some are dark
mysteries—full of questions and giving occasion to doubt.
Others are bright mysteries, things we do not understand, but
which enliven us with hope and courage.

Peter thinks of the truths he is sharing with us as "a lamp
shining in a dark place." He is writing at a time when it was
dangerous to be known as a follower of Jesus. He Himself
would face martyrdom in a short time. Others were being
hauled before unfriendly authorities and forced to give an
answer for their faith. Such dark times called for heavenly
light. And there is every evidence in the New Testament and
in the testimony of those first generation Christians that God
did give what was needed.

Paul goes perhaps a little further in this letter to the
Ephesians. He is very much aware of where those Ephesian
Christians had come from. They had not only lived in darkness—the darkness of paganism, "dead through trespasses
and sins in which you once walked" (Eph. 2:1, 2a)—but they
were so immersed in that life that they *were* darkness. "You
once were darkness." That's a sobering thought for us. When
we choose to live in the darkness of our self-chosen ways,

indulging the flesh, pride, jealousy, lust, greed or whatever, in a sense we *become* that darkness. It is not just something we put on, it inheres our souls.

There is a very encouraging thought, however, to hold onto. Darkness cannot overcome light. When light comes, darkness disappears. So when the light of Jesus Christ is operative in our soul, darkness cannot prevail. We "are light in the Lord." The positive statement is just as strong as the negative one. It indicates a radical change.

Are we aware of that great miracle operating in our lives today? Whatever the dark, mysterious place we are called to go through, we can bring light into it. That does not mean that we will understand it all. It does not even mean that we will be delivered from the temptation to doubt and despair. But we *have* light on the path: we have Jesus Christ indwelling in our souls by the Holy Spirit. He Himself said, "I am the Light of the world. He who follows me will not walk in darkness, but will have the light of life." (John 8:12)

Prayer: Almighty God, in whom is no darkness at all, grant us Thy light perpetually, and when we cannot see the way before us, may we continue to put our trust in Thee; that so being guided and guarded, we may be kept from falling this day, and finally, by Thy mercy, enter into our rest; through Jesus Christ our Lord. Amen.

(Professor Knight, 19th cent.)

1. What kinds of attitudes and actions allow darkness to creep into our lives?

2. What does the light of Christ bring into our lives?

Leaning on the Everlasting

Scripture: Deut. 33:26-27

*Text: The eternal God is your dwelling place, and
underneath are the everlasting arms. (Deut. 33:27)*

Some translations of the Bible render the term "dwelling
place" as "refuge." In either case, God is pictured as a
place of safety.

Life needs safe places. Even in our dreams we sense that
there are dangers abroad, and sometimes we catch a glimpse
of unseen but hostile forces at work in our world and in our
souls. Paul knew that when he lamented that in Himself he
could do no good thing. He had struggled with those unseen
and uncontrollable elements in his nature, and cried out, "O
wretched man that I am! Who shall deliver me from the body
of this death?" (Romans 7:24)

The Psalmist wrote, "Lord, thou hast been our *dwelling
place* in all generations." For the people of God, then and
now, God is our only safe dwelling place. Corrie Ten Boom,
the Dutch evangelist, used to say that if we wander into the
enemy's territory, we are fair game for Him. By that she was
emphasizing that our own safety is to stay *in Christ*. When we
deliberately sin, when we disregard what Jesus has told us, we
are like the careless Americans who "strayed" into Iraqi territory and spent several months in their prison. They did not
"know" that they were in hostile territory until they were
apprehended. On their release, one of them said, "I will not
go near the Iraqui border again."

We make this mistake spiritually when we begin to com-
promise with the world, when we begin to treat holy things
carelessly and callously. We leave the safe dwelling place God

has provided for us. When we make wise choices, denying the urge and impulse to "kick over the traces," we remain in that refuge He has provided. "Other refuge have I none; hangs my helpless soul on Thee."

Life "caves in" for all of us at times. It may be a combination of circumstances that we have to face that simply seem too much, too hard. "My foot had almost slipped," says the Psalmist. "Cast down, but not destroyed," echoes Paul. Every one of us gets cast down at times by events beyond our control. And here is where this wonderful truth comes into play: "Underneath are the everlasting arms." "Underneath!" It doesn't matter how low we may feel, it doesn't matter how hard a thing we have to face—there are the everlasting arms upholding us. We have a divine support that can never fail us. God will see to it that we have whatever is necessary to bring us through. He has pledged His word and will never go back on it.

Yesterday we talked about light on our path. Today we think about what is underneath that path: His everlasting strength and mercy.

"O how bright the path grows from day to day
Leaning on the everlasting arms."

Prayer: We thank You, Lord, that in all our needs, Your sustaining strength never fails. All our ways are known to you, and our desires and fears are not hidden from You. Grant us to know that underneath us today are the everlasting arms of Your mercy. In Jesus' name. Amen.

1. What internal and external influences are destructive to your spiritual life?

2. What is God's part in our spiritual battles?

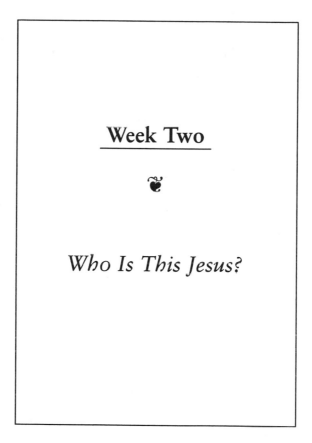

Week Two

❦

Who Is This Jesus?

Who Is This Jesus?

We will spend this week looking at who Jesus is. We are faced with many seeming contradictions: fully God, yet fully man . . . tempted in every way as we are, yet without sin . . . perfect and blameless, yet died a sinner's death on the cross.

Who *is* this Jesus Who loves us? The Bible has many glorious names for Jesus: Wonderful Counselor, the Prince of Peace, the Messiah, the Son of Man, the Son of God, Dayspring, the Rose of Sharon, the Living Water, the Bread of Life, the Good Shepherd, and the list goes on. But in asking *Who* Jesus is, we run into the question Jesus asked His disciples: "Who do *you* say that I am?" And that is the crucial question facing us.

Son of Mary

Scripture: Luke 2:15-21

Text: "Mary kept all these things, pondering them in her heart"
(Luke 2:19)

All this week we will be asking the question: Who is this Jesus who loves us? It is important to become better acquainted with Him, not only as a distant figure in the past, but as a present reality in our lives. But because His earthly life is where we see the human Jesus, the Gospels give us a composite picture to help us know who He was and who He is.

Beginnings and family lines are important. They determine in part not only how we look, but the way we talk and the way we think. Jesus was a Jew, born of a Jewish mother, and nourished in the traditions of Israel. We know from the Gospel account that Jesus was not only a Jewish child, born of a Jewish mother, but that He was also "conceived by the Holy Spirit," and that He was in very truth the Son of God. The Church has always held strongly to the truth that He was fully man, that is, fully *human*, and fully divine, that is, fully God.

Christians have also made much of His mother. Catholics and Orthodox traditions, harking back to the early centuries, have honored Mary as "Theotokos"—loosely termed "The God Carrier," or in more popular use, "the Mother of God." They were not claiming that Mary was anything other than a human mother, but that she was given the privilege and responsibility of bearing God's "only begotten Son." Jesus' humanity came through His mother, Mary.

Little is told us of her role in His childhood, so we are left to believe that, like any good Jewish mother of her time, she

22

would have trained Jesus "in the nurture and admonition of the Lord." We do know that when He began His ministry of teaching and healing, Mary "and His brethren" showed concern for Him, and there is every reason to believe that she accompanied Him on some of His missions. John records that she stood by His cross at the time of His death, and one of His last words were concern for her. Looking at John, the young beloved disciple, the dying Lord cried, "Son, behold your mother." And the evangelist says that John took her from that hour into his home. In the Book of Acts, we are told: "All of them [the apostles] with one accord devoted themselves in prayer, together *with the women and with Mary the mother of Jesus,* and with His brothers." (Acts 1:14)

According to a very old tradition, the service of Vespers in the Catholic and Orthodox churches, and the service of Evensong in the Anglican tradition include Mary's *Magnificat.* This is the song that is recorded in Luke 1. It bears similarity to Hannah's song after the birth of Samuel, when she took her child to "lend him to the Lord." (I Sam. 2:1-10) In the *Magnificat* Mary magnifies the Lord for all that He is doing for her in the coming birth of her Son. "For behold, henceforth all generations will call me blessed; for He who is mighty has done great things for me, and holy is His name." (Luke 1:49) It is altogether right and fitting that the Church, the new Israel, should continue to remember and honor the mother of her Lord. Over this writer's desk is an icon, a copy of "Our Lady of Vladimir," one of the most famous of the Russian icons. A sad-eyed mother is holding a little Child against her face. The little child has one hand clasping His mother's shawl and the other pressing against her face. It is for him a reminder that this mother not only brought her Son to birth, but loved Him and cared for Him throughout His life. Do the sadness of her eyes reflect what we read in today's Scripture: "Mary kept all these things, pondering them in her heart"? (2:19)

Prayer: Father in heaven, by Your grace the virgin mother of Your incarnate Son was blessed in bearing Him, but still more blessed in keeping Your word. As she pondered the mystery of Your love in her heart, may we, too, ponder the greatness of Your love in sending Your Son to be our Savior; we ask it in Jesus' name, who lives and reigns with You and the Holy Spirit, one God, for ever and ever. Amen.

1. What was the shepherds response when they saw the new born Jesus?

2. Why was Mary's response so different from theirs?

He Grew in Wisdom and Stature

Scripture: Luke 2:41-52

Text: "And he went down with them and came to Nazareth, and was obedient to them;" (Luke 2:51)

Where did we ever get the idea that as soon as we commit ourselves to Christ we should be spiritually "full grown"? The Greeks had a myth about the Goddess of Wisdom, Athena, springing full grown from the head of her father, Zeus. It seems that this idea of instant maturity is especially appealing to those who take their commitment seriously.

Counterbalancing this, Luke gives a little glimpse of the earthly life of our Lord Jesus Christ. Having told us of His miraculous birth, and those who had the insight to recognize what was happening, the evangelist then adds the one dependable picture we have of Jesus' childhood. What we see is not a wonder-worker (as was depicted in some of the later writings that did not get into the New Testament), but a child full of eagerness and curiosity to learn about God. Do you see the role of Joseph and Mary here? Not only in their taking Him with them to Jerusalem, but in their concern that He learn about the God of their fathers and the traditions of their people? Luke adds, after detailing the story of the boy Jesus in the temple, that "He went down with them and came to Nazareth, and was obedient to them." How else could He know what obedience meant without experiencing it Himself?

It is particularly interesting to note that this information must have come from Mary herself. "Mary kept all these things and pondered them in her heart." She knew that He was, in the words of the Creed, "conceived by the Holy Spirit." The angel had told her that the holy babe who was to

25

be born to her would be called "holy, the Son of God." So pondering these things in her heart, she knew a special responsibility rested on her. What it would all lead to she did not know. But day by day the task of training the holy Child was hers. In later years, the Lord quoted freely from the Scriptures. That meant that He had spent hours learning them as a child, and some of that learning must have been "at His mother's knee."

"The Holy Family" has been a favorite theme of artists over the centuries. The reason, I believe, is because in this way our Lord Jesus Christ draws near to us in a very down-to-earth, practical way. We, too, have to ponder in our hearts what it means to live and grow as children of God. We are not, like Athena, full grown at birth. Spiritually, there is a lot of ground to cover, a lot of learning and growing to be done. Jesus was willing to take time. God was willing to allot time for His Son to grow as a normal child, increasing "in wisdom and stature, and in favor with God and man."

Prayer: Help us, O Lord, to be patient with the process of spiritual growth. Help us not to think of ourselves as better, more mature, wiser than we ought to think. But like You, help us "grow in wisdom and stature, and in favor with God and man." We ask this in Jesus' name. Amen.

1. How would these Passover journeys have enabled Jesus to grow physically, mentally, socially, and spiritually?

2. What other means of growth were present in his life?

He Learned Obedience

Scripture: Hebrews 5:7-10

Text: "Although He was a Son, He learned obedience
through what He suffered.   (Hebrews 5:8)

This has always been a difficult verse for me. It becomes
even more difficult when the writer adds, "and being
made perfect. . . . " (v. 9a) What we have is a way of describ-
ing a living process, and my thinking has always tended to be
more "static." "If you're perfect, why do you say you are
being *made* perfect?"—that kind of reasoning. But here, as in
so many other places, the Scriptures move us into a different
realm. Absolutes without walls, you might say. We need (or as
least this writer needs) to allow more space for a mystery we
cannot fit into our little logical categories.

So here we have a perfectly obedient Son learning obedience through what He suffers. The New English Bible calls it
"the school of suffering." F. F. Bruce says, "We know the
sense in which the words are true of us; we learn to be obedient because of the unpleasant consequences which follow disobedience. It was not so with Him: He set out from the start
on the path of obedience to God, and learned by the sufferings which came His way in consequence just what obedience
to God involved in practice in the conditions of human life on
earth." And we know that for Jesus the cost of obedience was
very high indeed! Not only did it cost Him the rejection and
ridicule of His own people, but it eventually cost Him His life.
That price He paid at the end, having walked a life of daily
obedience from the beginning.

This says to me that, like Him, we will prepare ourselves
for the harder challenges by the small obediences of everyday

life. Those little things that are so easily forgotten, the small lies we indulge in, the neglects of the gentle nudges of the Holy Spirit, the cross words spoken and forgotten without repentance—these "little" disobediences eat away at the fabric of our souls, and weaken us for the big trials. On the other hand, as the old gospel song says, "Each victory helps us a victory to win." Learning obedience can mean learning that we grow spiritually when we are careful about the small as well as the big sins.

We do not need to flinch at the words, "He was made perfect," because it was the actual living-out of His obedience that fully qualified Him to be our Savior. His human life was not an accident, not a play-acting that was tacked on to an already foregone conclusion. It was a real human life, lived in obedience to the Father, sharing all the temptations and uncertainties we know—and yet, and *yet* fully obedient and perfect. And it was lived and given *for us*. That is the extent, the measure, the grandeur of the love of God. Yes! Jesus loves me!

Prayer: And we can love You, too, O Lord. How could we fail to love You, who have paid such a price of obedience and suffering—for our sakes? Amen.

1. What was Jesus' ultimate act of obedience?

2. What are the fruits of it?

Water and Dove

Scripture: Matthew 3:13-17

Text: "Cast your burden on the Lord, and He will sustain you;"
(Psalm 55:22)

Who is this Jesus who loves us? The Gospels tell us very little about His early life, leaving those thirty "hidden" years to intrigue the curious. What they do is to introduce us to the Man prepared to carry out His brief ministry that was destined to change the world.

Matthew tells us some wonderful things about Jesus' birth, and includes the story of the Magi who came seeking Him who was born king of the Jews. He also tells of Herod's cruel attempt to remove the threat of the newborn king's birth. Apparently the nature of tyrants has never changed, and there are examples even today of the same nervous, cruel jealousy operating in some parts of the world. But having told us those stories, Matthew is eager to get into the main message his Gospel was written to convey.

"In those days," says Matthew, "John the Baptist came preaching in the wilderness of Judea, 'Repent, for the kingdom of heaven is at hand.'" (chapter 3:1) The people knew that God had moved in the past to save His people, but now they lived under the iron yoke of Rome and its assigned representatives. John's message was a bold one: their future depended on their willingness to repent and turn to God. He even baptized those who responded to his message—symbolic of their need to be cleansed to be ready for the kingdom that was to come. Baptism was used at that time when a non-Jew wanted to embrace the Jewish tradition. By offering it to the Jews themselves, John was saying that their identity was not sufficient.

Repentance was necessary to qualify for God's kingdom.

Into this setting, with people coming from all directions to hear and respond to John, came Jesus. We know from the Gospel of Luke that John and Jesus were cousins. We also know that it is very likely that John the Baptist had been tutored by a community which existed in the desert east of the Jordan River. When Jesus appeared with those who were being baptized, John protested. "I have need to be baptized by you," he said, "and do you come to me?" It is clear that Jesus had no consciousness of sin, but that He had come to number Himself with those who have sin. "We do well to conform in this way with all that God requires," was His response. (New English Bible) Jesus was ready then, as He was throughout His ministry, to "conform with all that God required."

Since that time, those who follow Jesus have followed Him into the water of baptism. And since that time, we believe that God's Spirit also descends on those who thus obey the Lord. Baptism has become a meaningful and effective sign of our need. The dove which was seen descending and lighting on Jesus was a visible sign that God accepted and approved what His Son was doing. "You are My Son, My beloved, with whom I am well pleased." In that assurance our Lord began His public ministry. It would be a glorious but difficult one. The human Jesus needed to know that His path was meeting with the approval of His Father. That would be the thing that sustained Him to the end.

Prayer: Lord Jesus, You walked this earth in obedience to the Father's will. By Your grace and power, we too can walk in newness and obedience. By Your grace, enable us to walk with You today. Amen.

1. Why did Jesus come to John to be baptised?

2. What was the message of the Holy Spirit at this event?

The Son of Man — Messiah

Scripture: John 4:7-26

Text: Jesus said to her, "I who speak to you am He."   *(John 4:26)*

We can't get very far in thinking about who Jesus is without running into this term "Messiah." The Greek form of it is "Christ," and both words mean "anointed." There was a long-standing belief and hope among the Jews that the Messiah would come as their deliverer. He would be the descendant of David, whom God had promised would occupy his throne "forever." For instance, in Psalm 89, the Psalmist reminds God that He has said, "I will establish his line for ever and his throne as the days of the heavens." (verse 29) And again, "His line shall endure for ever, his throne as long as the sun before me." (verse 36) When Jesus came claiming to be the Promised One, He was considered by the leaders of His people to be a blasphemer and a false prophet. They thought they knew what kind of Messiah was to come, and He did not fit their expectations.

In what way *was* Jesus the promised Messiah? Certainly to claim that title for Him means to rethink what God has foretold in the prophets. There we see two images: one of a victorious King, coming to triumph over all that holds His people down. The other is that of a Suffering Servant, despised and rejected of men, "a man of sorrows and acquainted with grief." How can we reconcile such different pictures? Peter says that even those who prophesied did not fully understand what they were foretelling. "The prophets who prophesied of the grace that was to be yours searched and inquired about this salvation; they inquired what person or time was indicated by the Spirit of Christ within them when predicting the *sufferings* of

Christ and the *subsequent glory*." (I Peter 1:10 and 11) The Church has found what for us is the satisfactory answer. Jesus Himself, as He joined the disheartened disciples on the road to Emmaus that first Easter day said, "Was it not necessary that the Christ should suffer these things and enter into His glory?" (Luke 24:26) The suffering has been accomplished. The glory is yet fully to come.

When Jesus speaks to the Samaritan woman, telling her in all plainness that He is the one who was to come, He is setting aside all the human demands that God fulfill His promises in the way we expect. Like so many of His promises, we have to allow Him the freedom to fulfill them in His own way and wisdom. The Messiahship of Jesus has been one of those fulfilled promises, "a stumbling-block to Jews and folly to Gentiles, but to those who are called, both Jews and Greeks, Christ the power of God and the wisdom of God." (I Cor. 1:23, 24)

Coming to know who Jesus is means coming to know Him on His own terms. We cannot make Him in our likeness, though the temptation to do so is very great. We must learn to be honest before Him, listen carefully to what He tells us about Himself, and learn to read the circumstances of our lives in the light of who He is. He set aside the theological wrangling that the Samaritan woman tried to throw out as a way of avoiding Him. He will do the same for us if we allow Him. And as He did with her, He will tell us all that we ever did. (Cf. John 4:39)

Prayer: O most merciful Redeemer, Friend, and Brother: May I know Thee more clearly, love Thee more dearly, and follow Thee more nearly, day by day.

(Richard of Chichester, c.1197-1253)

1. How did Jesus' physical needs for rest and refreshment give him opportunity to meet another person's spiritual need?

2. How do drinking water and "living" water compare with each other?

Peter's Confession

Scripture: Matthew 16:13-23

Text: "You are the Christ, the Son of the living God."
(Matthew 16:16)

As we read the Gospels of Matthew and Mark, it seems clear that Jesus did not wish to go about announcing His identity to everyone. Instead, He waited for the twelve to come to understand who He was and how He was fulfilling His mission.

This is a famous passage, one in which Peter as the usual spokesman for the disciples, is first to recognize and say aloud the conclusion they had come to: Jesus was not just another prophet, not just a healer and worker of miracles. He was indeed the One who was promised, the Messiah, the Christ, the Anointed One. It is hard from our perspective to catch the full meaning of this for them, because "the Messiah" always had overtones of military deliverance and the setting up of God's Kingdom on earth. Jesus immediately encouraged Peter for his insight. "Blessed are you, Simon Bar-Jona! For flesh and blood has not revealed this to you, but my Father who is in heaven." Peter had been open to receive the truth, a truth that would be increasingly important to him and the others as time went on.

And then comes the "clinker." Knowing that the term would mean the wrong thing to them, Jesus immediately began to talk about His coming suffering and death. Whatever revelation Peter had had up to that point did not affect his reaction to this announcement. The Messiah must be victorious! The thought that Jesus might have to suffer and be killed was unthinkable. "God forbid, Lord!" was his answer. And the Lord, having just "complimented" Peter for his insight, now had to rebuke him for his lack of understanding. "Get behind me, Satan! You are a hindrance to me. . . . " (Matthew 16:23)

Peter was on the right track when he was able to recognize Jesus as the Messiah and as the Son of God. This would enable him to go out and proclaim the Gospel wherever he was sent. But he was on the wrong track in what he thought that would mean, and especially in thinking that the Messiah would not need to undergo suffering. He still lacked understanding of the mystery of Jesus' saving sacrifice. That would only become clear as he lived through the subsequent months and days.

Like Peter, we come to the Lord with a lot of preconceived ideas about what it will be like to follow Him. We like a cheerful Gospel, happy tunes, and victory rallies. We cringe and shy away from the call to walk through "the valley of shadows." So we begin where we are, and in His great mercy, He does not despise us. He knows that our understanding is very limited, but He says to us, when we recognize Him as Savior and Lord, "Flesh and blood has not revealed this to you, but my Father in heaven." We *are* on the right track. Then He has to lead us out of the "play-yard" of life's school and begin to teach us some of the harder lessons. In the process, our preconceived notions will be challenged and changed. Like Peter, we will come not only to know more fully who He is, but we will come to know more fully who we are. And that is one of the main effects that God is working in us as we walk with Him.

Prayer: Jesus, our Master, do Thou meet us while we walk in the way and long to reach the heavenly country; so that, following Thy light, we may keep the way of righteousness, and never wander away into the darkness of this world's night, while Thou, who art the Way, the Truth, and the Light are shining within us; for Thy mercy's sake. Amen.

(Mozarabic, tr. Wm. Bright)

1. How did Peter's concept of the Messiah differ from that of Jesus?

2. How can human understanding and care become impediments to God's purpose?

Who Do You Say that I Am?

Scripture: Mark 8:27-30

Text: "You are the Christ"   (Mark 8:29)

Today's Scripture is Mark's account of the conversation between Jesus and the disciples about who He was. Our best tradition ascribes the material in Mark's Gospel to the reminisces of Peter. That being so, it is significant that he omits Jesus' compliment about Peter's insight that Matthew includes in his version, but includes the rebuke that Peter received when he became a hindrance to the Lord.

We take a second look at this incident today, because, coming at the end of the week in which we were asking, "Who is this Jesus who loves us?" we face Jesus' question ourselves. He asked His disciples first, "Who do men say that I am?" and they began to give the various answers they were hearing. There were many different interpretations of what people were seeing and experiencing. Almost two thousand years haven't made a lot of difference in that respect. If we go out into the world asking people who they think Jesus is, we will get a variety of answers.

Some will say, "He was a great teacher." That is probably the most popular view, because it seems to pay Him respect without taking Him too seriously. As people get acquainted with His teaching, especially the parables and the Sermon on the Mount, they find it admirable. Pressed a bit further, they will also tell you that they think it is a bit extreme, impossible to keep. They would prefer that His teaching be toned down and made more practical. So, even acknowledging Him as a great Teacher, they proceed to dismiss Him. The word "Master," which we run into in the Gospels, means "Teacher," and suggests someone who is so highly regarded that his words are followed with great care.

Others will classify Jesus among the prophets. They will acknowledge that He had a very special relationship with God and that He broke new spiritual and religious ground. They respect Him as a founder of a strong and world-changing religion. But having said that, they would not acknowledge its having any spiritual authority over themselves. His religion is for others.

Then Jesus asks His disciples and you and me, "But who do *you* say that I am?" And that is the crucial question on which *everything* depends. Peter had no problem with his answer, nor did the others at that time. When you and I join Peter in making the same confession, "You are the Christ, the Son of God," we are giving Him our confession of faith and our pledge of loyalty. If Jesus is the Christ, the Son of God, your salvation and mine—in this life and the life to come—depend on our relationship to Him. John said it this way: "To all who received Him, who *believed* in His name, He gave power to become children of God." (John 1:12) Our simple faith in who He is unlocks the riches of heaven and admits us to the family of God.

> I know a life that is lost to God,
> Bound down by things of earth,
> But I know a Name, a precious Name,
> That can bring that soul new birth.

> *(Anonymous)*

Prayer: Enable us, O Lord God, to walk Your way with integrity and cheerfulness, faithfully believing Your Word and faithfully doing Your commandments, faithfully worshipping You and faithfully serving our neighbor; after the pattern and in the Name of Your Son our Savior Jesus Christ. Amen.

> *(Based on a phrase of Jeremy Taylor)*

1. Why is it important to know Jesus' true identity?

2. Why is it easier to think of Jesus as a teacher or prophet than as the Christ the Messiah?

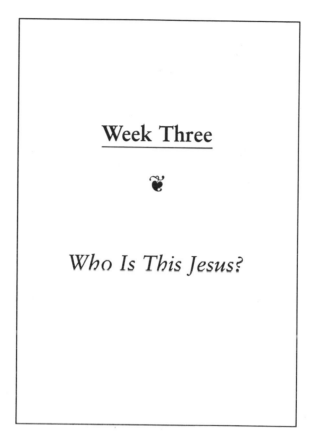

Week Three

❦

Who Is This Jesus?

Who Is This, That Even Wind and Sea Obey Him?

This week, we continue to pursue the question, Who *is* Jesus—and in doing so, we run into facing what Jesus asks of *us*. Part of the process of discovering Who He is consists of listening to what He says!

Jesus is so much larger than our problems. On the stormy Sea of Galilee, the disciples found out that there was much more to Jesus than they ever imagined! He is not bound by our fears and limitations, even though we are. Jesus calls us to lay aside our fear and trust Him. We need to *trust* Him in order to know Him.

We also need to remember that we are but dust, sinners in need of His saving grace. Part of the process of knowing Who Jesus is, lies in being obedient to what He commands us. Especially when we don't understand *why* we are being asked to do what we're being asked to do! This familiar old hymn perhaps puts it best:

> "Trust and obey,
> for there's no other way
> to be happy in Jesus:
> but to trust and obey!"

The Winds and Waves Obey Him

Scripture: Mark 4:35–41

Text: "And they were filled with awe, and said to one another,
"Who is this, that even the wind and the sea obey him?"
(Mark 4:41)

Who is this Jesus? Perhaps that was just what the disciples were asking themselves. They had witnessed some of His teaching, and had been with Him for many days. But they were only *beginning* to know Him. Campbell Morgan says, "This was a question of great fear. The statement of Mark, which our translators [KJV] have rendered, 'They feared exceedingly,' quite literally is, 'They feared with a great fear.'" And he goes on, "Moreover this fear was not produced by the storm, but by the calm. Whatever fear they had in the presence of the storm was lost as the greater fear and consternation took possession of them, when the storm was suddenly hushed and ended."

Fear is a common commodity of life. We know that it has its usefulness, but that it is often an enemy to be confronted and battled. Fear has many faces. We are afraid when we are threatened physically. We are afraid when an important relationship seems threatened. We are afraid of what others will think about us or say about us. And then there is *holy fear*. The Bible says, "But this is the man to whom I will look, he that is humble and contrite in spirit and trembles at My word." (Isaiah 66:2) And again, "The fear of the Lord is the beginning of wisdom." (Psalm 111:10)

The fear the disciples were experiencing here was the realization that they did not know this Man—that there were depths and dimensions, powers and possibilities within Him that they had not even imagined. Up to this time, their faith was a very limited one. And that is much like us. As we come to know Jesus, as we begin to trust Him, we are very likely to be easily thrown into panic and fear by the circumstances of life. Things "get out of control," and our natural reaction is to be afraid. In our fear, we may desperately try to save the situation, and only end by making it worse. Such has been the case in many incidents known to this writer.

At some point in our walk with Him, however, we are confronted by this magnificent, incredible fact: the winds and waves *do* obey Him. He is not limited by our puny faith, and we end up seeing, to our great amazement, that His way is always best. But this does not come all at once, and often we see it, only to lose sight of it when the next storm arises. How patient He is, even in His rebukes! As the Bible says, "He knows our frame. He remembers that we are dust."

Without this holy fear we are likely to presume on God. Without it, we are in danger of taking His mercy for granted. When He causes us to tremble inside, and reminds us that we are dust and that only He is God, then we are in better shape to get on with building a right and loving relationship. He wants us to believe in Him, to be sure of His goodness. He wants us to be calm in the face of life's storms. Are we willing to grow in that direction? It will mean confessing our fear over and over. It will mean acknowledging with shame that we have not trusted Him and asking for grace to trust Him more. But the grace will be there, and He will help us face the circumstantial fear if we treasure a holy fear of God.

Prayer: The winds and waves of life still obey Your voice, O Lord. May I remember that when they threaten my sense of security. Let Your word of peace calm every false fear today. In Jesus' name. Amen.

1. Contrast the disciples and Jesus' attitude toward the sudden storm.

2. What are the stormy events in your life that have brought fear and doubt?

We Know Who You Are!

Scripture: Mark 1:21–28

Text: "Let us alone; what have we to do with you, Jesus of Nazareth? Have you come to destroy us? We know who you are, the Holy One of God." (Mark 1:24)

We've talked about the slowness with which the disciples came to know and understand who Jesus was, and about our own slowness to comprehend. The demons had no such trouble. They knew immediately in whose presence they were.

The scene is the synagogue in Capernaum. Capernaum was Peter's home town, and later in the same day that this incident took place, Jesus and the others went to Peter's house. We have here a picture of how Jesus conducted His early ministry. It was apparently the custom that a "visiting rabbi" would be given an opportunity to expound some Scripture. Mark, in his usual brevity, simply says that Jesus "entered the synagogue and taught." Not many of us who are preachers have had our sermons interrupted by audible objections from the congregation. (They keep their objections to talk about later!) This writer does remember that in one of his first attempts at preaching (in the Philippines during World War II) a drunken native worker was playing cards in the audience, and caused quite an interruption. My response was less gracious and less powerful than was Jesus' reaction in this incident.

What do you make of the fact that this poor, trouble–filled man shouted out these words? To me it confronts us with the fact that life is always being lived on two levels, so to speak. There is the outward, "normal" level, the surface of things. Then there is the inner, hidden level where motivations and dark spirits vie for supremacy. Even pop–psychology teaches us that "things are not always what they seem," and that beneath what we see some very different things may be at work. The Scriptures do not go into any great explanation of the hiddenness of these demonic forces that work in the human soul. They show that both the Lord and the demons recognize each other. James says, "You believe in one God? You do well! The demons also believe, and tremble!" (James 2:19) A shallow belief that does not go to the heart of things is a devil's substitute for saving faith.

But look at this passage again. Jesus does not leave the poor man speaking for the devil. He knows what is needed, and He has indeed come to destroy the demonic power in that child of God. That is what He came to do: to destroy the work of the devil in the life of humankind. "For this purpose the Son of God was manifested, that He might destroy the works of the devil." (I John 3:8) Years ago a certain man sat in a Bible study in which this passage was being read. All of a sudden, it seemed, a new light broke on this passage. So much of the truth that seemed hard to accept about himself showed itself in this new light. For he had often felt that what was being said to him by others "threatened" to destroy him if he believed what they said. But it was as though Jesus were saying, "Yes, I have come to destroy the works of the devil in you. I have come to destroy that which destroys you. You do not have to fear looking at yourself in My light, because I came to save, not to condemn." And the man said, "I felt that I could hear people tell me where I was wrong in a way I had never been able to before."

I look at this passage as symbolic in some way, representa- tive of the "demonic" forces that work within us. Wherever we are deluded about ourselves and think better of ourselves than we should, wherever we cling to the idea that there is nothing but goodness inside us, we are playing the devil's game. How many times do we turn away, as this man wanted to do, because what we are seeing about *us* is too painful, and threatens to "destroy" us? This poor man in today's story did well to blurt out what he felt inside. It called attention to his great need, and Jesus, in His great mercy, met that need at that moment.

The winds and waves know His voice. The demons know, and tremble. Do we know? And are we ready to hear what He is saying to us?

Prayer: Grant, we beseech You, merciful Lord, to Your faithful people pardon and peace; that we may be cleansed from all our sins and serve You with a quiet mind; through Jesus Christ our Lord. Amen.

(Book of Common Prayer, alt.)

1. In this scripture passage, what two kinds of authority were exhibited?

2. Why were the people astonished?

A Friend of Sinners

Scripture: Matthew 11:16–19

Text: Jesus said, "The Son of man came eating and drinking, and they say, Behold a man gluttonous and a winebibber, a friend of publicans and sinners." *(Matthew 11:19)*

Who is this Jesus? As we continue to take a look at the portrait we have of Him in the Gospels, here is an important little glimpse of the way He was viewed by others. The "good" people of His day were scandalized by the company He kept. We know that there were many strict rules that controlled the behavior of the Pharisees. They avoided as much as possible contact with those they considered outside the umbrella of God's mercy. Their drive and goal was to keep themselves pure from defilement, and to cleanse themselves of any defilement they could not avoid. So it was a great scandal in their minds when this Teacher, this Rabbi, freely associated with "publicans and sinners."

There is a wonderful little story in chapter 7 of Luke's Gospel about a woman "who was a sinner" who came into a dinner being given for Jesus at the home of a Pharisee. When she learned that Jesus was there, she came in with an alabaster box of ointment, stood behind Him weeping, washed His feet with her tears, dried them with her hair, and anointed His feet with her precious ointment. The Pharisee was dumbfounded. "This man," he said, "if he were a prophet, would have known who and what kind of woman this is who touches Him, for she is a sinner." (Luke 7:39) The wonderful thing about that story is that Jesus *did* know who and what she was, and knew what was in her heart. In the same way, He knows who we are, and He does not despise our offerings.

When we shed tears of repentance, He does not belittle us. When we offer Him our love, incomplete and imperfect as it is, He does not reject it. He is still a friend of sinners, and He is still willing to receive the evidence that our hearts are turned toward Him.

Perhaps there is no more encouraging title given to Him, among the many that have been heaped upon His head, than this: He is the friend of sinners.

> Jesus, thou art the sinner's friend,
> As such I look to Thee.
> Now, in the fullness of Thy love,
> O Lord, remember me.

Prayer: Without any pretense of goodness on my own, with no excuses for my lack of faith and faithfulness, I look to You, Lord Jesus Christ, and trust in Your friendship and mercy. With thanksgiving for all You have done, I ask for grace to be a more faithful friend and follower, today and every day. Amen.

1. How were the marketplace children like the people that Jesus was addressing?

2. What is the final test of what is wise and true?

One Who Teaches with Authority

Scripture: Matthew 7:21–29

*Text: For He taught them as one having authority,
and not as the scribes.   (Matthew 7:29)*

As we think about the question, "Who is this Jesus?" we need to be careful to get the balanced picture of Him that the Gospels give us. There is so much in human nature that wants to make God a kind of Aladdin's "genie" who does our bidding, that we are in danger of using even those wonderful promises Jesus makes about prayer in the wrong way. We may be tempted to try to manipulate Him into doing our bidding instead of struggling to come into line with His will and purpose for us.

That is one reason why it is important to look carefully at this other facet of Jesus' nature in the Gospels. He does not come as one who is to be fooled or "fooled with." He strides into our lives as one with authority. In the last verses of Matthew's gospel, Jesus says, "All authority in heaven and on earth has been given to me." (Matt. 28:19) Early Christians understood this, and in the pictures of Jesus in the oldest churches that are still standing, Jesus is portrayed above the altar as "the Lord of the Universe." Sometimes they depicted Him with such a stern and penetrating face that he looks more like a judge than "the friend of sinners." But the point is an important one. He taught "as one having authority."

The authority Jesus displayed in His teaching came from His inner life, His communion with the Father. He was not out to prove Himself, to get something for Himself, not even to "win friends and influence people." He had one single motive: to fulfill the Father's will. That gave Him boldness, clearness, directness. You can see it in the Sermon on the Mount, and in every record of His teaching. He wastes no words, but speaks "heart to heart." He is about the Father's business. And that gave Him an inner authority that others could recognize and respond to.

The authority Jesus displayed enabled Him to reinterpret some of the hard sayings of Scripture. The scribes, on the other hand, were stuck in the traditions of the fathers, and lacked either the insight or the courage to shape them to any new understanding. Jesus said, "You have heard that it has been said, An eye for an eye, and a tooth for a tooth: But I say unto you, That ye resist not evil, but whosoever shall smite thee on thy right cheek, turn to him the other also. . . ." (Matt. 5: 38,39) "You have heard that it hath been said, Thou shalt love thy neighbor, and hate thine enemy. But I say unto you, Love your enemies, bless them that curse you, and do good to them that hate you, and pray for them which despitefully use you and persecute you; that ye may be the children of your Father which is in heaven. . . ." (Matt. 5:43–45) And in each case, he took a "legal" prescription and turned it into a spiritual principle. He went beyond behavior to address the spiritual condition of the heart.

The authority of Jesus is a guard against presumption on our part. If we listen to Him, he will direct us in the right path. Since His will is for our good, we cannot lose by allowing Him to have full reign over us. He comes, not to enslave, but to free; not to take life from us, but to give us life more abundant. How grateful we can be that "he teaches as one who has authority, and not as the scribes."

Prayer: We beseech Thee, Almighty God, look upon the hearty desires of Thy humble servants, and stretch forth the right hand of Thy Majesty, to be our defence against all our enemies; through Jesus Christ our Lord. Amen.

(Book of Common Prayer)

1. In today's parable, what does the rock represent?

2. During the windy, rainy seasons of your life, how has the truth of this parable been shown to you?

A Man of Sorrows

Scripture: Isaiah 53:3; Matthew 26:36–46

Text: Then He said to them, "My soul is exceeding sorrowful, even unto death." (Matthew 26:38a)

Who is this Jesus? "A man of sorrows and acquainted with grief." There is no true picture of Him if we leave out this part of the picture. Usually we think of His sorrows in connection with the final passion, the events leading up to His arrest, the betrayal of Judas, the desertion by the other disciples, the final torture, humiliation, pain, and death.

But there are other indications, too, of His ongoing sorrow. He wept at Lazarus' tomb. He was moved with compassion at the sight of the people who were scattered abroad, like sheep without a shepherd. He was disappointed in the lack of faith of the apostles, and said, "How long must I bear with you?" His life was filled with its sorrowful moments. We cannot believe that He went aside all night to pray without feeling something of the burden God had laid on Him in His earthly mission.

The Bible says, "We do not have a high priest who cannot be touched with the feeling of our infirmities; but was in all points tempted as we are, yet without sin." (Hebrews 4:15) And the prophet looking ahead, told of One of whom he could say, "Surely He hath borne our griefs, and carried our sorrows." (Isaiah 53:4)

Jesus' sorrows were part and parcel of His humanness. Any human being who does not know sorrow does not really know life. We are in a world filled with suffering and sin; injustice reigns and the innocent suffer. We are in a world of unexplained illness, where little children die "too soon" (according to our human feelings) and where cruelty is a way of life in many parts of the world. To be human, to be fully human is to know sorrow. It has ever been one of the great, central points of Christian belief that Jesus Christ, the Son of God, was also the son of Mary, a full and complete human being. We do not know how to reconcile these two realities, but we affirm that Jesus is Son of Man and Son of God. Our humanity is somehow wedded to God's divinity in this Man of Sorrows.

I do not know how you handle this truth in your life. For this writer, it is a reluctant admission that his thoughts and deeds must cause sorrow to the Savior. When given the grace of conviction and repentance, surely one of the things we see is that our cold heartedness, our spiritual deadness, our prayerlessness, our lack of thankfulness and our failure to love *must* cause sorrow to the One who loves us and sees all our ways. When we come to prayers of confession, it might be helpful to acknowledge that we have not only offended the Majesty of God and provoked His wrath (as the old prayers often expressed it), but that we have wounded the heart and love of One who cares. We may know personally what it feels like to have one's love trampled underfoot, ignored or rejected. To do the same to the Lord *must* cause Him sorrow.

> O Jesus, Thou art knocking,
>   And lo! that hand is scarred,
> And thorns Thy brow encircle,
>   And tears Thy face have marred.
> O love that passeth knowledge,
>   So patiently to wait!
> O sin that hath no equal,
>   So fast to bar the gate!
>   (*William W. How, 1867*)

Prayer: Almighty God, whose most dear Son went not up to joy but first suffered pain, and entered not into glory before He was crucified: mercifully grant that we, walking in the way of the cross, may find it none other than the way of life and peace; through the same Thy Son, Jesus Christ our Lord. Amen.

(Book of Common Prayer)

1. What appears to have been Jesus' purpose in bringing Peter, James, and John with him to Gethsemane?

2. At that place, what kinds of spiritual battles were to be fought?

WEEK THREE ❦ DAY 6

A Man of Joy

Scripture: Luke 10:21–22; John 15:7–11

Text: These things have I spoken unto you, that my joy might remain in you, and that your joy might be full.   (John 15:11)

Yesterday we talked about Jesus' sorrow and the importance of the fact that He knows His sorrow and ours. But there is that other side to Him that is also important. It is that He was a Man of joy and is a Man of joy. The old philosophers used to argue about whether God could *feel* anything. Some of them developed a concept of a God who could not be moved by any so-called "human" emotion.

But the Bible does not give us such a view of God. It speaks of His wrath, His anger, His pity, and even of His regret that He had made man at all! (Genesis 6:6) Correspondingly, it speaks of God's rejoicing. Zephaniah 3:17, speaking of Jerusalem, says, "The Lord thy God in the midst of thee is mighty; He will save, He will rejoice over thee with joy; He will rest in His love, He will joy over thee with singing." Psalm 104 says, "The Lord shall rejoice in His works." (verse 31) Today's reading reminds us of a time when Jesus "rejoiced in spirit." And we know that one of the criticisms leveled against Him was that he was "a winebibber." That does not indicate a man who was solemn, serious, and unable to laugh.

Yet joy, we know, is more than laughing. You can laugh at things that do not bring you joy at all. We may laugh instinctively when we fall down or someone else falls. Yet the fall may be serious. We laugh at jokes that have no real "joy" in them. Joy is something quite different from funniness. One can have joy even in the midst of great difficulties. One of the most profound statements I know about Jesus says, "for the joy that was set before Him, He endured the cross, despising the shame. . . ." (Hebrews 12:2) When we understand the root and source of Jesus' joy, we can better understand how our lives can add to His joy even today, and how His joy can be in us.

It seems to me that the one thing that we can do that will, if you please, increase the joy of God is to come into the place and condition He knows to be for our best. If you have children, you know that your joy in them is increased when they are most fully fulfilled—living active, useful lives of integrity and faith. It does not change our love for them when they fall, make mistakes or go astray. But it does affect our joy in them. Here is something that often escapes us. Just as we may choose to forget that our carelessness brings sorrow to our Savior, we may forget that when we find and obey His will, we increase His joy.

All that He has taught us, all that He has said to us has been done that His joy may remain in us, and that our joy might be full. It's little wonder that the hymn writer called it "great salvation": "Let us see Thy great salvation perfectly restored . . . " (Charles Wesley). Ours is indeed a "great salvation," for it leads us into the fullness of joy.

Prayer: Grant us, Lord, to rejoice in the things that bring You joy; to weep over those things that cause You sorrow; and to know the difference between them. In Your name we pray. Amen.

1. In the passage from Luke, what was the cause of Jesus' rejoicing?

2. According to John's gospel, how can we experience the joy of Jesus?

He Has Done All Things Well

Scripture: Mark 7:31–37

Text: They were astounded beyond measure, saying, "He has done all things well; He even makes the deaf to hear and the dumb to speak." (Mark 7:37)

The Gospels give us some wonderful glimpses of the earthly ministry of Jesus and the profound effect it had on those who witnessed it. Whether it was in the healing of the sick, the lame and the blind, or in feeding thousands of people from a few loaves and fishes, these miracles left the people agape with wonder. "We never saw it like this!" was one response.

Then they listened to His words. He did not speak in the usual fashion, "as the scribes," but spoke as one having an inner authority to say what He had to say. "No one ever spoke like this," was their response. And the Gospels add, "The common people heard Him gladly." When He spoke, it was to everyone who had ears to hear. No matter what walk of life a person might be following, His words penetrated to the heart of the matter. Even today, after two thousand years, His words still speak to the hearts of those who have ears to hear.

I find it still amazing that God has so accommodated our weakness and our needs as to send His Son to communicate His love and goodness to us. When we look at Jesus we see two things: we see what God is like and we see what human life is meant to be. Hebrews 1:3 says that He is "the express image" of God's person. So when we begin to know Him as He is revealed in Scripture and in our daily experience, we are really getting to know the Father. "He who has seen me has seen the Father," He told Philip.

When it comes to daily experience, however, we have to exercise faith in order to agree with our text. Things do not always seem to be working out as they should. Evil seems to get the upper hand, sickness befalls, dangers arise, disappointments confront us. In such circumstances some become bitter and turn away with the judgment that "a loving God would not allow such things." The Book of Psalms is a great help when we are going through a particularly difficult time (as well as other times!) because it encourages us to be honest with our feelings when we talk with God. When we think things are unfair, when we cannot understand "why," the Psalms invite us to lay our case before God. But even though we don't get the easy answers we'd like, we do get answers—sometimes like Paul, "My grace is enough for you." If we keep on *exercising* faith, we will come with heart and soul to say as did those witnesses to the miracles in today's text: "He has done all things well."

Prayer: Lord, we need a faith that will not shrivel up and run away when we are confronted with hard questions and unsolved problems. Your past faithfulness is enough to give us ground on which to stand, to believe, and to expect that which is best. Grant it for the sake of Your great name. Amen.

1. In what concrete ways did Jesus reach out to the deaf, mute man?

2. In what specific, personal ways has Jesus touched you in your times of need?

Week Four

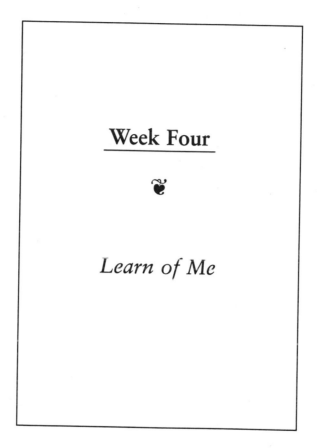

Learn of Me

Learn of Me

The problem with knowing who Jesus is, is that we want to make Him in our own image and to our liking. The cure, at least in part, is to search the Scriptures for the pictures we find there, not only in the four Gospels, but the reality of Christ in the Book of Acts and the epistles.

But it is important to correct our partial and sometimes distorted ideas of Jesus by going back to our divinely inspired records of what He said and did. This week we will use the Gospel of John as our source.

The Fourth Gospel is not like the other three. It is organized along very different lines, and does not seem to be particularly interested in a chronology of Jesus' life. There are no stories of the birth, but the incarnation of the Word is clearly described in the first chapter. There is no "secret" here of who He is or what He has come to do. Our evangelist is concerned as he says in the next to last chapter, "that you may believe that Jesus is the Christ, the Son of God, and that believing you may have life in His name." (John 20:31)

Along with a careful reading of the scriptural accounts, we need to pray for the leading and guidance of the Holy Spirit. Jesus said, "The Counselor, the Holy Spirit, whom the Father will send in my name, He will teach you all things, and bring to remembrance the things that I have said to you." (John

14:26) There will always be a mystery here that is larger and deeper than we can comprehend. But with the Spirit's help, we can learn more and enter more fully into that which God desires to show us. It is a worthwhile task and an exciting invitation. "Learn of Me," said Jesus. (Matthew 11:28)

The Bread of Life

Scripture: John 6:25-40

Text: Jesus said to them, "I am the bread of life; he who comes to me shall not hunger, and he who believes in me shall never thirst."
(John 6:35)

We begin this week's meditations with this great metaphor. Bread is the biblical word for food, and food is so basic to life that this becomes one of the most important words we have about who Jesus is.

In the Bible lands, bread is the staff of life. It is a synonym for food, and always carries with it the sense of what is basic and needed for survival. Here are some of the biblical references that will help us understand the significance of bread as the staff of life.

"When I break your staff of bread. . . ." (Lev. 26:26)

"When He summoned a famine on the land, and broke every staff of bread. . . ." (Psalm 105:16)

"Son of man, behold, I will break the staff of bread in Jerusalem . . . that they may lack bread and water. . . ." (Ezekiel 4:15,17)

". . . a land in which you will eat bread without scarcity. . . ." (Deut. 8:9)

The discussion of Jesus as "bread" carries us back to the Exodus of Israel from Egypt. As they crossed the Red Sea into the wilderness, it became evident very soon that they would have to receive divine assistance or they would soon starve. In answer to their need, "manna" was sent from heaven, and each day the people were instructed to go out and gather enough of it for that day. Only on the Sabbath could it be preserved and used a day after it was gathered. The Book of Psalms called it "food of angels."

In our Scripture today, Jesus speaks of "eating" this bread, and combines that thought with coming to Him and believing in Him. So we know that He is speaking of an inward receiving of something that gives and sustains life. He is speaking of the life of our souls or spirits, and reminding us that we cannot live on our own. We are not self-creating nor self-sustaining. Just as we must have bread, food, in order to maintain life, we must have the *spiritual bread*, food, in order to maintain our spiritual life.

In this generation of individualism and independence, it is a hard concept for many people to grasp. We do not easily think of ourselves as being constantly dependent on Jesus for daily, ongoing life. We rather think of Him as a Friend or Help. But this carries us further, deepens our involvement with Him, and urges us to take Him as daily food and drink.

In its celebration of the Eucharist or the Lord's Supper, the Church has always seen a special meaning in this great figure: the Bread of Life. "Beyond the sacred page, I seek Thee, Lord." Just as the food we eat becomes part of our bodies, the life, the very Bread of life, which Jesus gives us becomes a part of us. It is a mystery beyond our grasping, and we can only receive it by faith. But while we cannot *understand* it, we can live in its reality. Not only did Jesus say here in this text, "I am the bread of life," He sat at table with the twelve in the upper room, and "took bread and blessed, and broke it, and gave it to them, and said, 'Take; this is my body.'" (Mark 14:22) And when the disciples at Emmaus invited the Stranger who had walked with them on that first Easter day to stay with them, "He took the bread and blessed and broke it, and gave it to them. And their eyes were opened and they recognized Him." (Luke 24:30)

Prayer: Bread of heaven, on Thee we feed, for Thy flesh is meat indeed; Ever may our souls be fed with this true and living Bread; Day by day with strength supplied through the life of Him who died. Amen.

(Words by Josiah Conder, 1824)

1. What needs do earthly and spiritual bread meet?

2. Toward what does Jesus say that we should be directed?

The Water of Life

Scripture: John 4:1-14

Text: "Whoever drinks of the water that I shall give him will never thirst; the water that I shall give him will become in him a spring of water welling up to eternal life." (John 4:14)

Without water there can be no life. The bodies of plants, animals, and human beings are entirely dependent upon a continuing supply of it. And since the Bible comes to us out of a part of the world where water was both scarce and precious, it becomes a powerful spiritual symbol. The Psalmist says that the upright man shall be "like a tree planted by streams of water." (Psalm 1) David compares the Lord with a shepherd, and himself, a sheep. "He leads me beside still waters." That means safe waters where one can be renewed. We are told that the Hebrew word here is "He leads me beside the waters of rest."

Water also appears in the ministry of John the Baptist and the inauguration of Jesus' own ministry. In Luke's Gospel, John is quoted as saying, "I baptize you with water, but He who is mightier than I is coming. . . . He will baptize you with the Holy Spirit and with fire." (Luke 3:16) We see in this passage and in our text that "water" is a metaphor for the Holy Spirit. What is Jesus promising to the woman by the well, and to us? That His gift will be as vital to our spirits as water is to our bodies, and that the Spirit which He will give will "well up" to eternal life. Quite a promise!

Death and life have always been a source of curious wonder to human beings. What happens when life departs? What departs? When Jesus died, He cried, "Into thy hands I commend my spirit!" And there are many references in the Bible which describe death as the departing of the spirit. So a dead person is a *spiritless* person. Only the body is left. But what about a "walking dead man"? One who seems to be alive but is not? To the Church at Sardis the word came, "I know your works. You have the name of being alive, and you are dead. Awake, and strengthen what remains and is on the point of death, for I have not found your works perfect in the sight of my God." (Revelation 3:1b, 2) We have all felt it, I suspect—the condition of being "dead" inside.

But Jesus says that the water He will give will be like a well, spring up to eternal life. That's just the opposite of feeling dead and spiritless. The source of our "aliveness" is not ourselves, for we cannot *make* ourselves alive. The source of it is that living water, that moving, energizing, hope-giving Spirit which the Lord says He is ready to give.

A desert is a place that has been deprived of water for many years. Yet even the desert shall blossom and bloom when the refreshing rain falls on it. We can open ourselves to this live-giving Spirit if we see the need of it. If we feel dry and unfruitful, why not wait on the Lord and ask Him to send that Living Water into our souls? If we feel discouraged and defeated, why not look for the fulfillment of this promise? He is not playing games with us, and He is "always more ready to hear than we to pray, and to give more than we desire or deserve." So it is a safe risk to take.

The woman by the well must have heard with some part of her heart. She said, "Sir, give me this water, that I may not thirst, nor come here to draw." (verse 15) None calls Him in vain. And her imperfect request, I think, must have been transformed, so that she could long for and receive *the Living Water*.

Prayer: Lord, the refreshments of this world do not last. We get thirsty over and over again, and sometimes forget that You have promised that which will satisfy our deepest thirst. May we be more open to receive that Living Water, Your Spirit, and know that the well never runs dry. In Jesus' name. Amen.

1. Contrast the gifts given to the Samaritan people: those from Jacob and those from Jesus.

2. How are drinking water and "living" water similar?

The Light of the World

Scripture: John 9:1-12,24-25

*Text: Jesus spoke to them saying, "I am the light of the
world; he who follows me will not walk in darkness,
but will have the light of life." (John 8:12)*

All this week we are dealing with basic life metaphors—
bread, water, light. In our effort to better understand the
Jesus who loves us, we are listening to what He has to say
about Himself, seeking to understand better what these great
symbols mean to us.

Did you ever, as a child, turn over a rock to see what was
under it? There, in the darkness, you probably saw a number
of "creepy, crawly things." Years ago our family visited the
Bronx Zoo, and we found the reptile house especially fasci-
nating. In the display, you could pull out glass-covered
drawers, and there would be a serpent living in its dark, light-
less home. That somehow symbolizes to me what our souls
are like when we do not have the light of Christ within.

The Bible has two words to express the difficulty of finding
our way in the dark. There is the case of outer darkness (often
termed "night" in Scripture) and there is the case of blindness—the inability to *see* the light that is there. Jesus speaks
of the "blind leading the blind," and says, "If a blind man
leads a blind man, both will fall into the pit." (Matthew
15:14)

The story of this man born blind illumines our text today.
The disciples were like us. They were curious about the cause
of the man's condition, since he had been blind from birth.
They could not cure the blindness, but it was some satisfaction to know why it was there at all. Jesus' reply points up the

uselessness of such questions, and points their thoughts forward rather than backward. In this "age of pop analysis" we can spend a lot of time and energy trying to figure out "why" this or that condition is present, in ourselves or in others. Sometimes people make the mistake of rehearsing repeatedly some old insight about why they made wrong choices in their early life. "I'm trying to prove myself to my father . . . or mother . . . or . . . I've never felt acceptable to myself because I was not acceptable to my father . . . or mother . . ." And so on. Such repeating of old "insights" may become counterproductive. Can it not be, no matter how the condition came to be, that God will use it for His greater glory by allowing us to deal with it constructively? That's what Jesus seems to say about the blind man's condition. He was not so much interested in throwing light on the past as on the present and future possibilities which God was holding out to this man.

"I am the light of the world." That is a big claim! Yet as we look at Jesus, we can say, "Yes, Lord! You are the light of the world! You bring us truth about God—about grace, forgiveness, acceptance, and hope. You bring into this dark world what no one else has brought: the love that goes to the Cross; the resurrection that declares that death is not the end. With that light the world is brighter." The "sun of righteousness" has risen with healing in its wings.

There is an interesting thing about light and darkness. Darkness flees before the light. It cannot stand against it. When the light comes, darkness vanishes. So we can see that darkness is actually the absence of light. Do we prefer that absence? Are we afraid of His light? Do we want the healing that He holds out in the present and the future? These are questions that He raises when He comes as Light. "This is the judgment, that the light has come into the world, and men loved darkness rather than light, because their deeds were evil." (John 3:19)

Prayer: As long as You are present with us, Lord, we are in the Light. When You are present, all is well. Grant us grace to choose Your light over our darkness, and allow all the vain fantasies of the night to flee away before Your gracious presence; we ask it in Your name, who dwells with the Father and the Spirit in light everlasting. Amen.

1. In this episode, how are physical and spiritual blindness depicted?

2. According to vs. 24 and 25, what is the bottom line in this man's life?

The Good Shepherd

Scripture: John 10:7-18

*Text: I am the good shepherd. I know my own and my own know
me, as the Father knows me and I know the Father; and I lay
down my life for the sheep.   (John 10:14, 15)*

Do we begin to see that Jesus, the Jesus who loves us, is
too great to be contained with one or two metaphors?
How wonderful indeed it is that He comes to us laden with
these descriptions, to help us in our changing conditions!

The Shepherd image is too well known to need a lot of
explanation. But there are three thoughts in our text that bear
meditation:

First, Jesus is the *good* shepherd. Because people are not
always good, it is sadly true that some shepherds are not
good. They do not take good care of their sheep, or they may,
at times, be cruel to them. But the *good* shepherd takes
responsibility for his flock. Sheep are not known for their
super intelligence. The amusing movie, *Babe*, depicts sheep as
they are regarded by the sheep dogs, and as they regard themselves. The sheep dogs felt that sheep could only be controlled
by making them afraid. There are shepherds like that, too, I'm
sure. But David, the shepherd lad who wrote many psalms,
looked up to God as his Shepherd, and added, "Therefore I
shall lack nothing!"

Do we know this about Jesus? He has opened up the most
limitless possibilities to us in response to the prayer of faith.
"Ask and it shall be given you; seek and you will find; knock
and it will be opened to you." (Matthew 7:7) "Whatever you
ask in prayer, you will receive, if you have faith." (Matthew
21:22) This is the Good Shepherd talking. He means that we

shall have our needs met, "according to His riches in glory. . . ." (Philippians 4:19)

Second, Jesus *knows* His sheep by name. When we care about people, we learn their names. As long as they are just faces or bodies, we may not really care about them at all. But to name them gives them a personality of their own and a claim on our interest. Think of how much it means if you see someone after a long absence, perhaps of many years, and they smile at you and call you *by name*. When the Lord says, "I have called you by name, you are mine," He is saying that you are important to Him. The world disposes of people quickly—sometimes en masse. But God did not create us to dispose of us. He set a value on us, making us in His image, and sending His Son to become one of us. The Good Shepherd numbers Himself with us. He is both the Good Shepherd and the Lamb led to the slaughter *for our sake*.

But it is a little frightening to realize that we are known by name. Did you ever have the principal in school address you by name, and feel a little twinge of fear that you could not hide from him or her? You were known by name, perhaps by family, and that put a responsibility on you. It is not that different with the Good Shepherd. Knowing that He knows quickens our sense that what we are and what we do are not hidden from Him.

Third, the Good Shepherd *lays down His own life* to give us life. That is total, unqualified giving. Looking at Jesus after two thousand years, we may mistakenly think that, after all, He was the Son of God, and could foresee what would happen. But look at Him as a faithful young Galilean who had to walk by faith and prayer day by day to fulfill His mission. When He faced the cross, He prayed, "Father, if it is possible, let this cup pass from me." There were groans and sighs and tears. It was not a make-believe struggle, but a real one, and He did it for you. He laid down all that was dear for your sake and mine. That, ultimately, is why we are not afraid to go to Him and call upon Him in our deepest needs. He is the Shepherd who was willing to die for the life of His sheep.

Prayer: Lord Jesus Christ, who didst give all for us, help us to give all for Thee. Amen.

(Ernest Milner-White, alt.)

1. Compare the shepherd, the hired hand, and the thief.

2. What will unite the sheep that Jesus is calling to be in his flock?

The Resurrection and the Life

Scripture: John 11:17-27

Text: Jesus said to her, "I am the resurrection and the life; he who believes in me, though he die, yet shall he live, and whoever lives and believes in me shall never die." (John 11: 25,26)

Who is this Jesus who loves us? I am glad that He refuses to stay in the shallow places of my rational, materialistic mind! He keeps making statements like this and causing us to pause, wonder, search for the deeper meaning. Like the transfiguration scene on Mount Hermon, Jesus suddenly appears to be more than we had sensed Him to be. There the disciples saw His clothing become glistening white and they trembled with fear. That is a good and healthy balance to our tendency to make Jesus "one of us" in the wrong way.

Death is the last enemy to be destroyed, says the Bible. We are all fighting death in many ways. Some of us fight it by diets, medications, exercises, and programs. We may not *say* that's what we're doing, and we may not realize that's what we're doing, but I think that the "bottom line" is that we are trying to delay—or deny—death's power over us.

But we all die. That is an undeniable fact. The only question we have is this: will we look on death as a tragic end, cutting off all that is good and desirable? Will we look at others who die as having been robbed of their right to life? Or will we begin to let the awesome words our Lord speaks to Martha sink in and begin to defang the power of death?

Although these words were spoken before His own resurrection, we have the reality of Easter when we read them today. For two thousand years we have sung the victory of life over death. "O grave, where is thy victory?" We have heard these words read as loved ones were lowered into the earth, "in the sure and certain hope of the resurrection and the life of the world to come." And our hearts felt some comfort and peace in hearing them. But to appropriate them fully, we must *believe* the One who speaks them and *put our trust* in Him. The resurrection of the body awaits its time, but the resurrected life of which Jesus speaks here is a here and now experience. We can have new life even in these mortal bodies, a life that will never die.

In Romans 6, Paul uses baptism to illustrate this new life which Jesus gives. "We were buried therefore with Him by baptism into death, so that as Christ was raised from the dead by the glory of the Father, we too might walk in *newness of life*." (Romans 6:4) And I would venture to suggest that every day we can "walk in newness of life" if we keep open to Jesus, "the resurrection and the life." If His Spirit abides in us, we are constantly being kept alive for eternity. If His Spirit abides in us, we can make choices that are "life affirming." "Consider yourselves dead to sin," says Paul, "and alive to God in Christ Jesus." (Romans 6:11)

When Jesus tells us that He is the resurrection and the life, He is not setting us up to expect that life shall always be a bed of roses. Nothing in the Gospel would make us expect that we are going to live without problems, above all pain and perplexity. That is the common lot of mankind, and we are no exception. What He does is to give us a hope that will sustain us through our earthly, temporary losses, a present inner power to deal with the problems that come to us, and the assurance that "neither death nor life . . . nor anything else in all creation can separate us from the love of God in Christ Jesus our Lord." (Romans 8:32) Surely, surely, that is enough.

Prayer: Grant us, O Lord, the royalty of inward happiness, and the serenity which comes from living close to Thee: Daily renew in us the sense of joy, and let the eternal Spirit of the

Father dwell in our souls and bodies, filling us with light and grace, so that, bearing about with us the infection of a good courage, we may be diffusers of life, and may meet all ills and cross accidents with gallant and light-hearted happiness, giving Thee thanks always for all things. Amen.

(Lucy Soulsby, d. 1927)

1. According to this passage, what was Martha's understanding of who Jesus was?

2. At this moment what does the promise of eternal life mean to you?

The True Vine

Scripture: John 15:1-11

Text: As the branch cannot bear fruit by itself, unless it abides in the vine, neither can you, unless you abide in me.   (John 15:4)

Above my head as I write, there is a vine, a "Hoya" which some young friends gave me many years ago. Just yesterday I decided to break off a blossom which had gone past its prime. The scar that was left soon began to ooze a sticky substance from inside the vine, and I took a piece of kleenex and wrapped it to prevent its dripping. The vine has grown to an impressive length, twining itself in the blind by my desk and draping itself on the wall light fixture nearby. The branches are very healthy—as long as they stay anchored in the vine. If I were to sever them (which I have been tempted to do!) it would be only a short time before death would be visible, while the vine itself went on living.

This to me is what Jesus is talking about when He reminds us of who He is. The purpose of the branches is to bear fruit. The vine has life in it and its life can only be fully realized through the fruit-bearing branches. What are the hindrances to this process?

First, Jesus says, "If you keep my commandments, you will abide in my love." (verse 10) Disobedience is the sharp severance that separates us from the life of the vine. If we deliberately disobey, we can only expect the consequences of disobedience, not the blessings we want. This cannot be God's desire for us, because He has provided everything we need for fruitful lives, fulfilled lives. There is a struggle here that must be faced: the battle between our will and God's will.

Obedience is not only praying "thy will be done," but it is attempting, day by day and hour by hour, to live out that obedience. We have a lot of latitude in going about our daily lives, and it is easy to lose sight of words like this. It makes it all the more important to "check in" from time to time, and take a moment to see if we are on course.

Jesus again makes a breath-taking promise: "If you abide in me, and my words abide in you, ask whatever you will, and it shall be done for you." (verse 7) Henry Foster, a nineteenth-century physician, in his book, *Life Secrets*, says, "Our prayers must be a kind of happy labor to bring our desires into line with God's desires, so that His will can be done 'on earth as it is in heaven.'" Abiding in the vine means sharing the same life-goal as the vine itself. And since we know that many of our goals and desires and dreams are *not* just in line with His, that makes our prayer vital, genuine, even energetic. Jesus means to be the life-flow in us, so that our lives can be part of God's overall purpose and plan.

The third thing that Jesus says to us about His role as vine and ours as branches is found in the last verse of today's Scripture: "These things I have spoken to you, that *My* joy may be in you, and that *your* joy may be full." To His disciples in the Garden before His crucifixion He said, "In the world you may have tribulation, but be of good cheer, I have overcome the world." (John 16:23) We are called to bear the marks of the Vine. We are enabled to bear the marks of the Vine. We have the inflowing life, supplying our need, producing fruit to His praise and our joy—*if* we continue to abide in Him.

Who is this Jesus who loves us? Closer than breathing, nearer than hands and feet. He is the inner life of our life, giving us all that we need today, and tomorrow, and the day after.

Prayer: O Lord our God, You are the life within our life. Without You we wither and die, and come to nothing. But with Your life-giving life, we can grow and find fulfillment in bearing fruit to Your praise and glory. May it be so today, we ask in Jesus' name. Amen.

1. In this metaphor what is Jesus' relationship to the Father and to his followers?

2. What does God intend for us in this kind of relationship?

I and the Father Are One

Scripture: John 10:22-30

Text: I and the Father are one. *(John 10:30)*

When we ask ourselves the question, "Who is this Jesus?" we always come back to this: He was more than a man. He was One who came from above and brought with Him the aura of heaven. His robes were "all fragrant with myrrh and aloes and cassia . . . out of the Ivory Palaces." (Psalm 45) When men heard Him speak, as the poet said, "Something in His countenance I would fain call Master." He drew women and men, not only to Himself, but to something beyond Himself—to the Land of Beginning, to the Place from which we had fallen in the long ago.

This Jesus breathed the air of eternity, and those who walked and talked with Him soon began to realize, albeit imperfectly, that they were made for something better than tax collecting and fishing. Tax collecting and fishing might be needed, but they cannot be the total meaning of life, and this is what Jesus came to help them see. "Blessed are the . . . poor the needy . . . the merciful . . . the peacemakers . . . the pure in heart." Blessed are those who begin to catch a vision of what this Love came to bring.

It did not take the disciples long after the resurrection to realize that when they had converse with Jesus they had converse with God. "I and the Father are one," He had said, and they didn't know what that meant. We still don't know all it means. Sometimes we may speak to "Jesus," and sometimes to the "Father," and sometimes to the "Spirit." But, even though we do not understand it, it doesn't bother us, because we know in our hearts that in all cases we are dealing with God, the holy and undivided Trinity.

But Jesus gives us a human face, a likeness to ourselves to which we can relate. We are not talking to a great invisible, cosmic "Force" but to a Person, a Friend, and Brother, one who has made Himself one of us. This is the Jesus who loves us and wants us to learn to love Him more and more. It would be frightening indeed to be in a universe in which we could only sense power and mystery. But when we know that at the heart of this universe, no matter what mysteries may remain, there is One who loves us, whose name we know, and who calls us by name, fear flees and faith grows.

Prayer: Jesus, our Master, do Thou meet us while we walk in the way, and long to reach the Country; so that, following Thy light, we may keep the way of righteousness, and never wander away into the darkness of this world's night, while Thou, who art the Way, the Truth, and the Life, art shining within us; for Thine own name's sake. Amen.

(Mozarabic Liturgy)

1. What appears to be the reason for the Jews' demand for Jesus to define himself?

2. What characterizes the sheep that belong to Jesus?

Week Five

❦

Tell Me the Old, Old Story

Tell Me the Old, Old Story

This week we will concentrate on the Greatest Story ever told, and look at it in a variety of ways. In doing this, we will use words from some of the songs sung by generations past, which may be passing out of use in our day.

Katherine Hankey was the daughter of a well-to-do English banker. She was affiliated with a dedicated group of Christians known as the Clapham Sect, which included William Wilberforce, John Newton, and Hannah More. This group was active in the effort to abolish the slave trade, the extension of missionary efforts, especially in India, and the establishment of the British and Foreign Bible Society. Miss Hankey, like Hannah More, was active in starting Bible classes for girls and had a keen interest in missionary work. In 1866, after a long illness, she wrote a poem from which the words of this hymn were taken. William H. Doane heard the words read at a convention in Montreal and was so moved by them that he secured a copy of the words, took them to the White Mountains, and composed the tune to which it is sung.

Tell me the old, old story, Of unseen things above,
  Of Jesus and His glory, Of Jesus and His love;
Tell me the story simply, As to a little child,
  For I am weak and weary, And helpless and defiled.

Tell me the old, old story, (3x)
Of Jesus and His love.

Tell me the story slowly, That I may take it in,
 That wonderful redemption, God's remedy for sin.
Tell me the story often, For I forget it soon,
 The "early dew" of morning, Has passed away at noon.

Tell me the story softly, With earnest tones and grave,
 Remember, I'm the sinner, That Jesus came to save.
Tell me the story always, If you would really be
 In any time of trouble, A comforter to me.

Tell me the same old story, When you have cause to fear
 That this world's empty glory, Is costing me too dear.
O yes, and when its glory, Is dawning on my soul,
 Tell me the old, old story: "Christ Jesus makes thee
 whole."

As to a Little Child

Scriptures: Mark 10:13-16 and Matthew 11:25,26.

Text: Truly I say to you, whoever does not receive the kingdom of God like a child shall not enter it. (Mark 10:15)

"Tell me the story simply, As to a little child; For I am weak and weary, and helpless and defiled."

The Bible makes a big point of the difficulty the wise have in accepting and receiving the Gospel. It declares in effect that man's wisdom is contrary to God, and at enmity with Him. Human learning easily leads to pride and rebellion. Something in our nature that wants to believe the serpent's first lie, that we can disobey and still "be like God, knowing good and evil."

And so, in His loving kindness, God comes to us another way. He invites us to set aside our favorite opinions, our self-excusing rationalizations, and become "as little children." Children can learn many, many things because they do not think they know everything. Not only so, but children are ready to believe what we tell them unless we have betrayed their trust.

Nicodemus is a good example of a "wise" man who was confused by Jesus' words. The conversation recorded in John 3 ends with Nicodemus' question, "Can a man enter his mother's womb and be born over again?" We can believe that he thought further about these things, because he appears later on as a believer and friend. But at the time, becoming "like a little child" seemed almost too difficult for him.

The hymn writer says she is "weak and weary and helpless and defiled." Let's look at those thoughts. Do you feel "weak and helpless" in any situation? Are you confronted by problems too complex or too intransigent for you to solve? Then you can identify with the song. Paul was an energetic, capable man. But he had something that plagued him and he pleaded with God to take it from him. The answer came, "My grace is sufficient for you. *My* strength is made perfect in weakness." Our weakness can be the very gift that God gives to make us open to His greater blessing. Our strengths can keep back what He would choose to give if we were more needy.

Are you "weary"? That word suggests toiling and striving, putting forth effort to get something done. It is related to "wear and tear." Sometimes we say, "I'm worn out." But the writer is not speaking just of being tired at the end of a hard day. It is something more serious. This is spiritual weariness, a feeling that we aren't getting anywhere. Again, Paul warned the Christians in Galatians and Thessalonica, "Let us not grow weary in well-doing. . . . " (Gal. 6:9) That kind of spiritual exhaustion has led many people to abandon their walk with God, and to drift into a kind of no-man's land of godlessness. But our song says that there is a remedy for this!

Finally, that word "defiled" is used to describe our condition. It is not the innocence of childhood, but the defilement of later life—the defilement caused by wrong thoughts and choices. The word suggests impurity, debasement, even corruption. So it is a serious description of our need for cleansing and purifying. Where can such a miracle take place? The Gospel. The old, old story. Here is where we find renewal, regeneration for flagging spirits, and cleansing for all the stains of life. Every day a miracle is offered, including this one. Can we receive it "as a little child"?

Prayer: Thankful that we can turn to You as little children, Father of all goodness and mercy, we ask that the miracle of renewal and cleansing be worked in us today. In the name of Jesus Christ our Lord. Amen.

1. What was Jesus' response to the children who were brought to him?

2. In order to receive the truths of the kingdom of God, why is a child-like attitude necessary?

Our Forgetfulness

Scriptures: Hebrews 2:1-3a and 2 Timothy 2:8-15

Text: Therefore we must pay closer attention to what we have heard, lest we drift away from it. (Hebrews 2:1)

Tell me the story often, For I forget so soon!
The early dew! of morning has passed away at noon.

There is an old story about a minister who kept preaching the same sermon over and over again, until the lay officers came to him and asked him why he didn't preach something new. His answer was, "You haven't practiced what I'm telling you in this one yet!"

A wonderful teacher who meant a lot to this writer used to say, "I haven't anything new to say today." And she would go on to rehearse many of the same truths she had spoken again and again. She was making sure that the hearers did not fail to hear the basic spiritual truth that had been entrusted to her.

Is this what the hymn writer had in mind with that request? And is this why our Lord made *one* request, that whenever we break the Bread and drink the Cup that we do it "in remembrance" of Him? Christians cannot afford to get far from that simple, life-changing truth.

The phrase "early dew" of morning may seem strange to our generation. The prophet Hosea says to His people, "Your love is like a morning cloud, like the dew that goes early away." (Hosea 6:4) Jesus talked in His parable about the seed that sprang up quickly, only to fade with the heat of the day, because it had no deep root. These are warnings to us that the early, sometimes exciting feelings we may have in our walk with the Lord tend to fade away. If we neglect that which is vital, the promised fulfillment will never come.

This very exercise in which we are engaged is intended to counter this forgetful tendency that is in us all. By a simple commitment to read the Scripture and these thoughts, to spend some time in reflection and prayer, we are choosing *not* to neglect our great salvation. We are choosing to counter the impatient, rebellious spirit within us that is ever seeking new things, and bringing our minds back to the source of life and growth. It is in such homely means as this that the Lord meets our need and helps us to stay closer to Him.

"I forget so soon!" says our hymn. As we grow older, we do indeed forget quickly many things: where we left our keys, why we have just come into the pantry, even what we had for dinner yesterday. And yet, for most of us, along with the failure of our short-term memory, we recall clearly many things in the distant past. That seems to be a part of the way God has allowed life to be. I like these words of Maltbie D. Babcock:

> This is my Father's world: Oh, let me ne'er forget,
> That though the wrong seems oft so strong,
> God is the ruler yet!"

There are many things today that will tempt you to forget that God is the ruler yet. But if you remember Jesus, if you think on the way He is at work in your life, then you will find a source of strength for every trial and every trouble. That is His promise. Only, don't forget to remember!

Prayer: Father, we need to be reminded often of who we are and of Your love for us. When we forget You, we go astray into many harmful directions. So of Your great mercy, continue to prod our minds awake and keep our memory of Jesus fresh, even as we walk with You; we ask this in His name. Amen.

1. According to the passage in Timothy, what is the essence of the gospel?

2. What was the clear focus of Paul's life?

Thou art the Man!

Scripture: 2 Samuel 12:1-9a

Text: [David] said to Nathan, ". . . the man who has done this deserves to die. . . . " Nathan said to David, "You are the man!"
(2 Samuel 12:5b and 7a)

Tell me the story softly, With earnest tones and grave;
Remember! I'm the sinner, Whom Jesus came to save.

The point of the story of Nathan and David is that David was quick to see the sin in another, but that he had to be confronted to look at his own sin. Psalm 51 bears as its heading, "A Psalm of David, when Nathan the prophet came unto him, after he had gone in to Bathsheba." And that psalm is one of the most beloved and most frequently used psalms in the entire psalter. "Have mercy on me, O God, according to Thy loving kindness. . . . Wash me thoroughly from my iniquity and cleanse me from my sin." (Verses 1a and 2) David is called "a man after God's own heart," and that in spite of his grievous sins of adultery and murder. The secret seems to lie here: his fear of God and his willingness to repent.

If our real needs are to be met, we must be addressed at times "in earnest tones and grave." Our problems cannot be healed lightly if they are to stay healed. A "quick fix" often turns out to be no fix at all. Our spiritual problems and needs run deep, to the very core of our being. We are complex creatures, hardly understanding ourselves at all. Even Paul, for all his spiritual insights and accomplishments, confesses, "I do not understand my own actions. For I do not do what I want, but I do the very thing I hate." (Romans 7:15) Since God knows this about us, and since He knows how we try to hide even from ourselves the worst about ourselves, He patiently keeps on telling us "the old, old story."

It is good to think about what it cost God to enter our human life on His saving mission. Not only do we read about His word coming through the prophets and teachers throughout the Old Testament, but when we get to the Gospel the conflict between the darkness and the light grows very intense indeed. Jesus' suffering was not confined to Good Friday. After all, He was born in a stable, a sign that He is entering at the lowest point of human need to bear the burden of the world's sin and rebellion. When He died on Calvary, even the heavens shut their face from Him, and the sky was darkened at noon. Our salvation is not a cheap "fix." It is "so great a salvation," wrought with infinite cost by our heavenly Father and His only begotten Son. Why was so great a price paid? Because our need was so great.

"Remember! I'm the sinner that Jesus came to save." When we can say that, our hearts overflow with gratitude too great for words. As Isaac Watts says, "Love so amazing, so divine, demands my life, my soul, my all!" Remembering renews that sense of wonder, love, and gratitude that enables us to keep on the path.

Prayer: Father, the Good News still stirs our hearts and quickens our faith. We know that without Your grace and mercy we are left to flounder and stumble in the darkness of this world and of our own sinful natures. And so we thank You, praise You, and glorify You, knowing that the Gospel was meant for us. In Jesus name. Amen.

1. How were David's actions a sin against God as well as against his neighbor?

2. How was Nathan's confrontation an act of responsibility toward God, his king, and his people?

Christ Jesus Makes Thee Whole

Scripture: Acts 4:1-12

Text: Be it known to you . . . that by the name of Jesus Christ of Nazareth . . . this man is standing before you well. (Acts 4:10)

Tell me the same old story when you have cause to fear
That this world's empty glory is costing me too dear;
Yes, and when its glory is dawning on my soul,
Tell me the old, old story: "Christ Jesus makes thee whole."

There are two themes in this stanza worth looking at: the temptation of the world to pull us away from our first love, and the power of the Gospel to make us well and whole.

First, the pull and temptation of the world. We all know what that is, for we all live with it. Is our generation more exposed to that pull than others have been? We are bombarded on every side by "the media"—television, radio, newspapers, magazines—all holding up their invitation to us to please ourselves. One particularly offensive TV ad ends with the words: "You're worth it." The world's pull is based on the same temptations that have always been present. There are no new ones. But they come to us packaged in the form of stories, advertisements, talks, editorials, even slanted "news" items. The glory of the world is dressed as attractively as possible, and something in us responds positively to it. Much of it seems good, and it is easy to forget that it is "empty glory." Very recently we were treated to many news items about the auction of the estate of a very famous person. People paid huge sums to own something that had belonged to her or her husband. The "emptiness" of some of their comments is a sad comment on how beguiled many people are. One buyer wished to be buried with the object she purchased at the auction!

What we need to ask ourselves, and the Holy Spirit of Truth, is this: when is the "empty glory" of the world costing us "too dear"? Have our eyes been blinded to the real values and priorities? Are we chasing "will-o-the-wisps" and using our energy for things that amount to nothing? The prophet asks: "Why do you spend your money for that which is not bread, and your labor for that which does not satisfy?" (Isaiah 55:2) Yet if we are honest, we have to admit that much time and energy is spent in "that which does not satisfy." Another hymn writer says it this way: "From the best bliss that earth imparts, we turn *unfilled* to Thee again."

One clue to the answer to this question is this: how long does the satisfaction last? Someone has said that when the applause stops, it takes only a few minutes until the hunger for it arises again in the performer's heart. How long does peace remain in your heart in return for your labor and effort? Someone close to this writer used to work hard and long at preparing things for her family's Christmas. But inevitably, something would happen to spoil the whole scene, and the one who had worked so hard and so faithfully would end up hurt rather than happy. If we are finding such frustrations, is it not time to ask, "Is it costing me too dear"?

The second point this stanza is making has to do with what can draw us back from the deadly fascination with the glory of the present age. It is, says our song, "the old, old story," that "Christ Jesus makes thee whole." Our text and Scripture expand this concept of "wholeness" to include the "here" as well as the "hereafter." God *is* concerned about our wholeness, physical, emotional, and spiritual. So there is nothing to be ashamed of in praying about our physical problems and to expect His healing hand to touch our needs.

There is a world of difference between setting out to get free from some bad habit—some addiction—for the sake of our pride and ambition and seeking the same goal in order to

94

become more obedient children of God and better witnesses to Him. In the first case, the desire is simply to become freer to pursue our own selfish goals. The second results in thankfulness and praise. You could say the difference between "programs" that have to do with weight loss or other addiction problems can be seen in this very point.

But God *does* care. God *is* for you. And the wonderful words are still true: "Christ Jesus makes thee whole." His healing hand is still extended toward your need and mine. *That* is the "old, old story!"

Prayer: Heavenly Father, for the blessings we have already received, for Your present help in our need, and for Your promise for all that we shall need, we give You our heartfelt thanks through Jesus Christ our Lord. Amen.

1. Contrast the fruit of what the world offers, with what Jesus promises to give us.

2. In this scripture passage, how was the fruit of the Spirit shown in the lives of Peter and John?

Wonderful Words of Life

Scripture: John 6:63-71

*Text: Simon Peter answered him, "Lord, to whom shall we go?
You have the words of eternal life."   (John 6:68)*

Sing them over again to me, Wonderful words of life;
Let me more of their beauty see, Wonderful words of life.
Words of life and beauty, teach me faith and duty;
Beautiful words, wonderful words,
Wonderful words of life.

Philip P. Bliss, 1874

The Psalmist prayed, "Thy word have I laid up in my heart
that I might not sin against Thee." (Psalm 119:11)

Ours has been called a religion of the Book, and the very
term "God's Word" is one of the most important concepts we
have. It is the foundation of our faith that God has spoken to
us and that we can know Him through what He has said.
Even our Lord Jesus Christ is called "The Word" who was
with God and shared God's divine nature from the beginning.

P. P. Bliss wrote this little song in celebration of the Word
of God in 1874, two years before his death. It is not a distin-
guished piece of poetry, but it has undoubtedly served a good
purpose in helping people think about and celebrate the gift
of God's "wonderful words of life."

Peter spoke for the whole group when people were finding
Jesus' words too hard. He had made the statement that He
was the Bread which came down from heaven to give life to
the world, that if "anyone eats of this bread he will live for
ever; and the bread which I shall give for the life of the world
is my flesh." (John 6:51). That was too much for them to take

in. Like us, they tended to be quite literalistic and prosaic, and were not interested in having something that deep and mysterious thrown at them. So they walked away. "This is a hard saying; who can listen to it?" And so Jesus turned to His disciples, asking, "Will you go away also?"

But Peter and the others had listened to Him day by day. They had walked with Him. They had seen Him heal the sick, drive out the dark demonic powers, and they had caught a vision, imperfect as their understanding still was, of something so great that they could not give it up, even if they could not fully comprehend it. "O love, that wilt not let me go!"

Have we heard those wonderful words of life? Have we felt the quickening of faith, hope, and love as we hear about God's care? Do we see in the Lord Jesus an acting out on the human plane of something far beyond human telling? Does the Holy Spirit quicken those words to us, and quicken us with them? They are indeed "words of life."

Death is a good description of a life from which God is shut out. Death means separation, isolation, hopelessness. But the "wonderful words of life" ushers in a new reality. Just as Jesus came forth from the tomb, our souls arise at the beckoning of the word of life. We are "re-born" as we are quickened by the life-giving Word. "Talitha cumi; Little girl, I say to you, arise." (Mark 5:41) His words are still "wonderful words of life"!

Prayer: How firm a foundation You have given us in Your Word, O Lord. May I find new life and new hope in it today; for the sake of Him who is Your Word, Jesus Christ our Lord. Amen.

1. Describe the kind of life that comes through words given by the Spirit.

2. How can we become more receptive to God's word?

The Ninety and Nine

Scripture: Luke 15:2-7

Text: And when He has found it, he lays it on
his shoulders, rejoicing.   (Luke 15:5)

There were ninety and nine that safely lay
In the shelter of the fold,
But one was out on the hills away,
Far off from the gates of gold.
Away on the mountains wild and bare,
Away from the tender Shepherd's care.

"Lord, Thou hast here Thy ninety and nine;
Are they not enough for Thee?"
But the Shepherd made answer,
"This of Mine Has wandered away from Me.
And although the road be rough and steep,
I go to the desert to find My sheep."

But none of the ransomed ever knew
How deep were the waters crossed;
Nor how dark was the night that the Lord passed through
Ere He found the sheep that was lost.
Out in the desert He heard its cry—
Sick and helpless, and ready to die.

"Lord, whence are those blood-drops all the way
That mark out the mountain's track?"
"They were shed for the one who had gone astray
Ere the Shepherd could bring him back."
"Lord, whence are Thy hands so rent and torn?"
"They're pierced tonight by many a thorn."

But all through the mountains, thunder-riven,
And up from the rocky steep,
There arose a glad cry to the gate of heaven,
"Rejoice! I have found My sheep!"
And the angels echoed around the throne,
"Rejoice! for the Lord brings back His own!"

Elizabeth Clephane was plagued with illness for many years before her death in 1869 at the age of thirty-nine. Her poems, including this one, were published in Scotland after her death. It was first sung by Ira D. Sankey at a rally with D. L. Moody at the Assembly Hall in Edinburgh, and the tune was composed extemporaneously by Sankey as he sang. "When I reached the end of the song," Mr. Sankey said later, "Mr. Moody was in tears and so was I."

"Rejoice!" is the word for today. It is God's word over every one who repents and turns in heart-felt repentence to Him. The only way we can gladden the heart of God is to enter into His joy with our own. Ours is a joy-filled way when we walk with Him. The Shepherd still hunts and finds us in our wounds, our sicknesses, our sorrows, and our fears. And He still carries us over those places that are too hard for us. Surely we can know that "The Lord is my shepherd, I shall lack nothing!" He is still in the business of taking us from our lostness to His light, from our sickness to His health. "Rejoice!"

Prayer: As there is joy in heaven over one soul that repents and turns to You, Lord, there is joy in our hearts when we find Your forgiveness and grace. Amen.

1. Who is the lost sheep?

2. In this parable, how are God's feelings described?

Coming Home

Scripture: Luke 15:11-24

Text: I will arise and go to my Father. (Luke 15:18)

Softly and tenderly Jesus is calling,
  Calling for you and for me,
See, on the portals He's waiting and watching,
  Watching for you and for me.

Refrain:
Come home, come home, Ye who are weary, come
  home;
Earnestly, tenderly Jesus is calling,
Calling, O sinner, come home!

Oh! for the wonderful love He has promised,
  Promised for you and for me;
Though we have sinned, He has mercy and pardon,
  Pardon for you and for me.

Will L. Thompson

We may think of this song as intended more for those who have not made a first commitment to Christ, for certainly it has been used as an "invitational hymn" for generations since it was written. But we would do well in this context to see how it fits with the story of the Prodigal Son, and how it relates to our own lives in a practical way.

There is a yearning for home in all of us. Even when we are at home, we are not fully satisfied, for we are still "banished children of Eve," in exile from our true home in God. As perfect as our earthly homes may be made, they always leave something to be satisfied. That is as it should be. Earth's blessings could become chains to bind us here if there was not still a thirst which they cannot satisfy.

It is good to remember that the yearning for home is a God-given gift. It is a part of the mercy of God that leaves us thirsty for Him. The prodigal, like so many of us, thought little of that. The pleasures of youth, and the prospect of even more pleasure loomed so large in his mind that he thought little or nothing of the consequences of his decisions. Alas! how many of us have followed that path, in great or small ways. We have seized the world by the tail, so to speak, and determined to have our way, get what we wanted out of life. It does not necessarily mean that we sought the same route as did the prodigal, who "wasted his substance in riotous living." Our wanderings may have been much more respectable, guarded, and conventional than that. But the inward result would have to be the same. When we have strayed far from the Shepherd's fold, far from the Father's house, we inevitably end up broken in heart and spirit, hungering for true Bread, and longing for home.

Heaven, The Heart's True Home is the title of a very helpful book by Peter Kreeft, a professor at Boston College. He makes the point over and over again that, since we are created for life with God and in God, we will always be unfulfilled until we arrive at our intended destination. Knowing this, we can face the necessary disciplines, challenges, and delays that help to prepare us for going home. The prodigal was unprepared for the grace he met when he arrived back at his father's house. Are we, too, not surprised to find how gracious our heavenly Father is as we turn from our wanderings? His grace is still amazing!

Prayer: Thyself, O my God, Thyself for Thine own sake, above all things I love. Thyself as my last end I long for. Make me therefore in this life present always to love Thee before all things, to seek Thee in all things, and at the last in the life to come, to find and to keep Thee for ever. Amen.

(Thomas Bradwardine, 1349)

1. In what ways have we wandered from our Father's home?

2. According to this parable, how would you describe the Father?

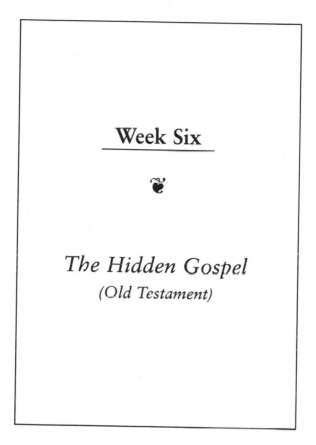

Week Six

❧

The Hidden Gospel
(Old Testament)

The Hidden Gospel

As we continue this venture of seeking to know better the Jesus who loves us, we turn this week to what the Old Testament Scriptures say about Him.

These Scriptures have been called "the hidden Gospel," because they are found in very unexpected places throughout the Old Testament. Sometimes we know that the words themselves carried at least two meanings—one that applied to the immediate historic situation in which they first came, and then, as the people of God reflected on them, they came to see in them a wider, and more far-reaching meaning. From the days that the Gospels themselves were written, right on through the early centuries of the Church, these wider, more far-reaching meanings were studied and treasured.

Jesus Himself is our authority that these Scriptures testified or bore witness to Him. Before He came as a little child in Bethlehem, there were the signs hidden away waiting for believing hearts to treasure them. When Herod was visited by the wise men, for instance, he called in "the chief priests and scribes of the people," who told him that the Messiah, the Christ, would be born in Bethlehem, "for so it is written by the prophet: And you, O Bethlehem, in the land of Judah, are by no means least among the rulers of Judah; for from you

shall come a ruler who will govern my people Israel."
(Matthew 2:5, 6)

There is a little verse in I Peter which can help us as we look at these Old Testament Scriptures.

"The prophets who prophesied of the grace that was to be yours searched and inquired about this salvation; they inquired what person or time was indicated by the Spirit of Christ within them when predicting the sufferings of Christ and the subsequent glory." (I Peter 1:10, 11)

In other words, the prophets were not given to understand completely what they were prophesying. So it is not surprising that their words are found "hidden" among prophecies that relate to another time and situation. It took the full revelation of Jesus and the enlightenment of the Spirit to bring together these wonderful words of promise and hope.

They Called Me "Emmanuel"

Scripture: Isaiah 7:14

Text: Therefore the Lord Himself will give you a sign.
Behold, a virgin shall conceive and bear a son,
and shall call His name Immanuel."

The word "Emmanuel" appears in the Old Testament only twice: in this verse and in the next chapter. The context is not a cheerful one, for the prophet is foretelling that King Ahaz has, in a sense, sealed Judah's doom by his faithlessness. But here, in the midst of the "bad news," comes this word: a sign will be given (even though unsought) and the child's name will be called "Emmanuel," which means "God with us."

When Matthew wrote his inspired account of the birth of Jesus, this verse shed light on it, and the writer saw that the wondrous birth had actually been dimly forecast in this Isaiah passage. And so we inherit this powerful description of the nature of Jesus. When we call Him "Immanuel," we are affirming the fulfillment of this prophetic promise. The Virgin has conceived and born a son, and we call Him "Immanuel."

There is a mystery about Jesus which we can never fully understand. In His divinity He is fully human, and in His humanity He is fully divine. As a man, we see Him grow tired, hungry, sad, joyful—even discouraged. As the Son of God we see Him manifesting the works of God and challenging the entrenched power of the devil. Both are necessary to our full appreciation of who Jesus is. "Emmanuel" sums up both at once. He is with us, as one of us. And He is "God with us."

Christians throughout the centuries have found in this name a source of comfort and hope. Here are some of the ways we see Immanuel used.

O come, O come Emmanuel. (Hymn based on the Great O antiphons sung in monasteries for seven days before Christmas.)

O come, O come, Emmanuel, and ransom captive Israel;
Who mourns in lonely exile here, until the Son of God appear.

> Oh! Christ He is the Fountain,
> The deep sweet well of love!
> The streams on earth I've tasted,
> More deep I'll drink above.
> There to an ocean fullness
> His mercy doth expand,
> *And glory, glory dwelleth in Emmanuel's land.*

John Bunyan in his immortal classic, *Pilgrim's Progress*, has this beautiful passage, symbolically representing Christian maturity as a "place," "Immanuel's land."

"Christian and Hopeful continued on their way till they came to the Delectable Mountains, which belong to the Lord of that hill of which we have spoken before. So they went up to the mountains to behold the gardens and orchards, the vineyards and fountains of water. There they drank and washed themselves and freely ate of the vineyards.

"Now there were on the tops of these mountains Shepherds feeding their flocks, and they stood by the side of the highway. The Pilgrims went to them and asked, "Whose Delectable Mountains are these? And whose are the sheep that feed on them?" "These mountains are Immanuel's Land," replied the Shepherds. "And they are within sight of His city. The sheep are His, too, and He laid down His life for them."

Prayer: O come, Emmanuel, God with us, and abide with us throughout our earthly journey. Amen.

1. In this pasage of scripture, what is the significance of the child,
   Immanuel?

2. How does the knowledge that God is with you affect your life?

They Called Me "Prince of Peace"

Scripture: Isaiah 9:2-7

Text: . . . and His name will be called . . . Prince of Peace."
(Isaiah 9:6)

The story of God's people throughout the Old Testament is the story of war. They were conquered over and over again, and spent much of their history as vassals of foreign governments. But the promise of a time of peace stayed alive in their hearts, and visions of the prophets confirmed that God's promise would one day be fulfilled.

"My people will abide in a peaceful habitation, in secure dwellings, and in quiet resting places." (Isa. 32:18)

"Behold, I will bring it health and cure, and I will cure them, and will reveal unto them the abundance of peace and truth." (Jeremiah 33:6)

"I will make with them a covenant of peace and banish wild beasts from the land, so that they may dwell securely in the wilderness and sleep in the woods." (Ezekiel 34:25)

When Jesus came, He came to fulfill the hopes and promises that the generations had treasured. There were very few who still held on to the hope, for so long they had dwelt under the power of stronger nations. But the Gospel of Luke introduces us to several of them: Zechariah and Elizabeth, parents of John the Baptist; Anna, the aged prophetess in the temple, and Simeon. (Luke 2:29, 20)

Since Israel's history was a history of war, the most logical way of visualizing "the peaceable kingdom" was political: the lion and lamb lying down together. But even in the prophets there had been an indication that another kind of peace was to be sought. Isaiah said, "Thou wilt keep him in perfect

110

peace whose mind is stayed on thee." (Isaiah 26:3) The peace Jesus came to give was more than a ceasefire. "My peace I give you," He told His disciples. "Not as the world gives do I give to you." (John 14:27)

Think about those words as you think of Jesus as the Prince of Peace. It is a special kind of peace He brings. "*My* peace I give you." If we are looking only for the kind of peace we want, the kind we think would be the answer to our trouble, we may overlook, or even reject His peace. His peace sometimes comes with a disturbance that stirs up fears and tears. When that happens, it does not mean that the Prince of Peace is failing us. It is that the process of bringing *His* peace involves such a preparation.

> Peace, perfect peace, our future all unknown?
> Jesus we know, and He is on the throne!
>
> *(Edward H. Bickersteth, 1875)*

Prayer: O Prince of peace: You will ordain peace for us—in Your own time and way. Help us to look for it, expect it, wait for it, and rejoice in it. Amen.

1. Contrast the characteristics of the promised child with the prior description of the gory residue of war.

2. List the promises of hope that are given in this passage.

They Called Me "Savior"

Scripture: Zephaniah 3:14-20

Text: The Lord thy God is in the midst of thee; He will save, He
will rejoice over thee with joy, He will rest in His love, He will
joy over you with singing.   (Zephaniah 3:17, KJV)

This is clearly a Messianic promise. Spoken during the
reign of Josiah (640-609 BC), the prophet warns that the
corruption of the nation was leading to certain ruin. Belief in
magic and in the power of other gods had become wide-
spread. A great falling away from true faith in the Lord God
had taken place. So the prophet has the burden of announcing that the Day of the Lord would come, but it was not
something to look forward to with glad heart. It would be a
day of wrath and punishment. God's righteousness would not
be mocked. His people had refused correction, and now they
had sealed their own punishment.

What a lesson for us at this time in our history! In spite of
all the religion that is prevalent, we have forsaken the way of
the Lord in many serious ways. Unless there is a turning back,
it is clear that we are sowing to the wind, and can expect to
reap the whirlwind. It is a time for repentance, prayer, and
intercession. Some among us tell us that it is too late, and that
we can expect the "Day of Wrath" to come upon our generation.

As we think about who Jesus is, and His love for us, we
need to hear the hope contained in todays' text. "He will
save." Jesus said, "God sent His Son into the world, not to
condemn the world, but that the world might be saved
through Him." (John 3:17) It seems that God is always look-

ing for those who are willing to be saved, looking for "an opportunity," if you will, to perform a saving work. "I have no pleasure in the death of anyone, says the Lord God, so turn, and live." (Ezekiel 18:32)

The question comes, then, How does Jesus save? That term "save" has its roots in a Latin term that means "safe." It is also related to "health," "wholeness," "wellbeing." So an answer to our question, How does Jesus save? involves our whole being, body, soul, and spirit. When we awaken to faith in Jesus as our Savior, we become aware that He has saved us from the penalty of all our wrongdoing. Our separation from God has been healed, and we are "safe" in the family of God. Our exile is over, and we are on our way home. That, to me, sums up the great truth about what Jesus has done, is doing, and will do in our lives.

> Perverse and foolish oft I strayed,
> And yet in love He sought me,
> And on His shoulders gently laid,
> And home, rejoicing, brought me.
>
> *(H. W. Baker, based on Psalm 23)*

Prayer: Keep the vision before my eyes, most blessed Lord, of Your rejoicing over one lost sinner who is found and saved. May Your saving grace effect in me all that I need to enter into the joy of the Lord. In Jesus' name. Amen.

1. What does this passage tell us about the heart of God?

2. How can this knowledge be an encouragement to us in the uncertainties of our lives?

They Called Me "Son of David"

Scripture: Isaiah 11:1-10; 9:7

*Text: In that day the root of Jesse shall stand as an ensign
to the peoples; Him shall the nations seek, and His
dwellings shall be glorious.   (Isaiah 11:10)*

When the Magi asked Herod, "Where is he who has been
born king of the Jews?" Herod immediately summoned
the scholars to find out where the Messiah was to be born.
Their immediate answer was, "In Bethlehem." Bethlehem was
the city of David, and the Messiah would be "of the house
and lineage of David." When the angel messengers gave their
word to the shepherds in the field, they said, "To you is born
this day in the city of David a Savior, who is Christ [the
Messiah] the Lord." (Luke 2:11)

God said of David that He had found in him a man after
His own heart. There is much in David's life that reveals his
weaknesses and his human frailty. But over and above it all,
there is tremendous testimony that this man truly loved God
"with all his heart." The promise that God gave to him was
that one would sit on his throne forever. As prophet after
prophet arose to rebuke the people for their sin and to renew
God's promises and God's call, they spoke of this abiding
promise: God would raise up one on the throne of David to
rule His people.

As we look at who Jesus is in the light of these predictions,
it is another way of confirming that God keeps His promises.
There was no earthly way to figure out how God was going
to bring to pass what He had said. After all, the people had
been so faithless that they were finally carried away into
Assyria and Babylonia as slaves. The great kingdom of David

and Solomon had become a "hissing and an everlasting reproach." (Jeremiah 25:9) We read in psalm after psalm the sorrow the people felt. "O God, the heathen have come into Thy inheritance; they have defiled Thy holy temple; they have laid Jerusalem in ruins." (Psalm 79:1) As for Israel, her hopes were fallen to the ground, and she could say, "There is none to help."

That is the way God works. When we have gone to the depth of failure and despair, He remembers His promises. Even when we have earned the fears and anxieties that plague us, God does not forget us. Jesus, the Son of David, is born in the little forgotten town of Bethlehem. While the world is busy with a thousand "important" things, God goes quietly about His work.

You can see it in your life as I can in mine, if you open the eyes of faith. Whether your story is a dramatic one, or just "garden variety," it is still true. His promises are sure and faithful, and Jesus, the Son of David, the Son of God stands ready to help.

Prayer: Thank You Lord, for Your faithfulness to me, when I have lost my faith, and when all seems empty and I am alone. Open my eyes of faith that I may see You, fulfilling Your promises, and preparing the way.

1. According to Isaiah 11:1-5, what will the promised king be like?

2. In the following verses what does Isaiah say will happen during his reign?

They Called Me "Redeemer"

Scripture: Isaiah 59:14-22

Text: And He will come to Zion as Redeemer to those in Jacob
who turn from transgression, says the Lord. *(Isaiah 59:20)*

To better understand Jesus as our Redeemer, let us look at what the dictionary says about the meaning of the word, "redeem." **1:** To buy back, repurchase; **b.** to get or win back. **2:** to free from what distresses or harms; **a.** to free from captivity by payment of ransom, **b.** to exticate from or help to overcome something detrimental, **c.** to release from blame or debt: clear, **d.** to free from the consequences of sin. **3:** to change for the better: reform. **4:** to repair or restore.

As we have said several times in these meditations, Israel was often captive to other peoples in the area. It was numerically outnumbered by stronger nations—Egypt, Assyria, Babylon, to name a few. Even the tribes of people who were left when they came into Canaan sometimes overran and overpowered them. So they knew what it was to live under hostile domination. One passage of the Old Testament pictures the Israelites hiding in caves and going out to till their fields, hiding their grain from the enemy. So the promise that one would come to Zion as Redeemer had real meaning for them. He would be the one who would free them from captivity, from slavery, and His coming would bring in a new era of peace and tranquility.

This promise was part of the Messianic hope. The Messiah would be the one who would come and restore the fortunes of Israel, and the days of David and Solomon were recalled as the happy time when God was on the throne and Israel was a praise and glory to Him. The Messiah would be the Anointed

King. Sometimes he is pictured as a strong hero, and at other times He is seen as something more than human. When the Old Testament was translated into the Greek language, the term "Christ" was used to mean "The Anointed One," "the Messiah."

We cannot fully understand Jesus and His relation to us without the use of this great figure, Redeemer. He comes to rescue us from our fallen estate. He comes to reclaim us from all that is detrimental to our welfare, to change us for the better, to bring us to the place where God created us to be. That is His intention in entering our lives. But it is more than that. He comes prepared to pay the price. And the price is His own life, His blood. So eager is He to see us back in our divinely intended condition that He is willing to go the full length, to hold nothing back to secure our welfare and our salvation. He comes as Redeemer to claim us for Himself.

"You know that you were not redeemed with corruptible things, as silver and gold . . . but with the precious blood of Christ, as of a lamb without blemish and without spot." (I Peter 1:18,19 KJV)

> I will sing of my Redeemer, and His precious love to me;
> On the cross He sealed my pardon, paid the debt and set me free!

Prayer: Most gracious Lord, You did not hesitate to give all that we might be brought back to God. Accept my thanks and praise for Your great love, and grant me grace to honor You in all that I do. Amen.

1. What was the situation described in verses 14 and 15, and how did God feel about it?

2. According to verses 16-22, what were the results of God's response to this situation?

117

They Called Me "Prophet"

Scripture: Deuteronomy 18:15-22

Text: Moses said, "The Lord God will raise up for you a prophet from your brethren as He raised me up. You shall listen to Him in whatever He tells you."   (Acts 3:22)

To say the least, this is one of the most unique sermons ever preached. Peter was speaking to the people in Solomon's portico of the Temple after the healing of the lame man. The crowd was curious as to how Peter and John were able to make the lame man walk and run. It was Peter's opportunity to tell them about God's gracious action in their behalf. And so he began to tell them how Jesus had come in fulfillment of all that the prophets had written and promised. Although Jesus had been killed, God had raised Him up from the dead, and He was now the Author of life, and through faith in His name the lame man stood "in perfect health" before them all. With the "live evidence" right there, Peter's sermon had to have a life-changing effect on his hearers.

Twice in the Book of Acts this same Scripture from Deuteronomy is quoted: "The Lord God will raise up for you a prophet from your brethren." The prophet was a man who spoke for God. The priest was a man who represented the people to God. But the prophet often brought a message of "bad news" about God's coming judgment. Often people did not wait to see if his words were coming true. They found them offensive and thought the best way to get rid of them was to get rid of the spokesman.

Jesus applied the term "prophet" to Himself. He said, "A prophet is not without honor, except in his own country, and among his own kin, and in his own house." (Mark 6:4) As He set His face toward Jerusalem He said, "It cannot be that a prophet should perish away from Jerusalem. O Jerusalem, Jerusalem, killing the prophets and stoning those who are sent to you! How often would I have gathered your children together as a hen gathers her brood under her wings, and you would not!" (Luke 13:33b, 34)

Jesus' work as a prophet was in telling the great news, "The Kingdom of heaven is at hand!" He announces a new day, a new time, a new reality in God's dealings with mankind. Ever since the day He first went out to preach, we have been in that new time. The kingdom of heaven is at hand! God has spoken through the mouth of His Prophet. He has declared that He is doing a new thing. Salvation is now being offered to people of every kindred, race, and tribe. This is the divine message our Lord Jesus, the Prophet, has brought to us.

When Jesus preached His prophetic message, He said, "Repent and believe the Good News." That is the twofold challenge of the prophet. If what He is telling us about ourselves is true, we need to repent, to change, to turn toward God. But the turning is toward "the Good News." Believing the Good News is believing that God so loved us that He sent His Prophet to announce that the door of the Kingdom is open to us, that the Father's love reaches out to us, and that we can become more truly, day by day, children of the King. Repent and believe the Good News!

Prayer: Lord, we sometimes turn away from You for fear that You will bring us bad news. Forgive us that we listen to fear instead of Your loving invitation to life. This day I choose life. May Your word find lodging in my heart and bring forth fruit for Your praise and glory. In Jesus' name. Amen.

1. How did God's way of speaking differ from the practices of the nations that were dispossessed by the Israelites?

2. How does God speak to us today?

They Called Me "King"

Scripture: Zechariah 9:9-10; Micah 5:2-4

Text: Lo, your king comes to you; triumphant and victorious is He, humble and riding on an ass, on a colt the foal of an ass.
(Zechariah 9:9b)

Even in this age of democracy, the word "king" carries a special sense of majesty and authority. We are told that the root meaning of the word "king" is "one who is able." In the Old Testament, God was called "King" of Israel, and until the people demanded of Samuel that he anoint a king for them, there was no person in Israel who carried that title. The people were united under the kingship of God, and the various tribes were ruled by chieftans. When the whole nation was in need of special leadership, a judge was raised up to deliver them and to become a focal point for the life of the people. Some of the judges were Gideon, Deborah, Samson, and Eli.

After the choice of Saul as the first king of Israel, Samuel became aware that Saul had disqualified himself through his disregard of God's instructions and his disobedience. "Because you have rejected the word of the Lord," Samuel told him, "God has rejected you from being king." It then became Samuel's delicate task to find and anoint a successor to Saul. The story of how David was chosen and what developed under his reign is one of the great sagas in the story of Israel. From David's time on, the term "king" evoked images of his reign. He was not only a man after God's own heart, he was also the ideal king.

As Israel suffered enslavement by foreign nations, prophets like Zechariah and Micah held out the promise that one day

121

God would send another king. They always thought of that promise in terms of David's kingship. So it is significant when blind Bartimaeus cries out to Jesus for help that he addresses Him as "Son of David." It shows that the hope of the coming King was still alive in the hearts of many people, and David was the pattern of the king they hoped to see.

When the Scriptures foretell that a king would come "lowly and sitting on an ass," they are picturing the coming of a peaceable kingdom. His coming would be a sign of peace, not of war. And His kingdom would be one where the lion and lamb would dwell together.

A prayer which pious Jews used in this period went like this: "May He establish His kingdom during your life and during your days, and during the life of all the house of Israel."

As we think about the Scriptures' promise, and about how our Lord fulfilled them, the question for us is this: are we prepared to live as children of the kingdom? Are we willing to allow the King to have His way with us, especially when His way crosses ours.

Prayer: O Lord Jesus Christ, King and Savior, may Your kingdom come and Your will be done in me this day. Amen.

1. According to today's scriptures, how would you describe the promised king?

2. How does this king differ from others?

Week Seven

❦

They Testify of Me
(New Testament)

They Testify of Me

Some New Testament testimonies.

Last week we looked at some of the ways the Old Testament seers and prophets foretold the coming of our Lord Jesus Christ. They did not always understand what they were foretelling, and certainly did not have a full picture of the one who was to come. But their visions and their words kept hope alive in the hearts of the faithful. The New Testament writers, especially the Gospel writers, found in these words a kind of hidden Gospel before the Gospel. They lifted them out and up, and with the facts of Jesus' life, they help us see how God mysteriously moves to confirm His word and strengthen our faith.

This week we will look at the testimony of a number of people whose lives intersected that of Jesus—or, to say it more accurately, whose lives were intersected by our Lord. What they saw and what they gave witness to can help us better understand who this Jesus is who loves us.

The Witness of Simeon

Scripture: Luke 2:25–35

Text: Lord, now let your servant depart in peace, according to Your Word; for mine eyes have seen Your salvation! (Luke 2:29,30a)

Simeon was an old man, one of the faithful ones who had not forgotten God's promise. He was "looking for the consolation of Israel."

We know that Judea had been under foreign domination for centuries at this time. First the Greeks, then the Romans came in with their superior military power, and little Judea was no match for them. Judea lay in the way of these strong empires, and they could not afford to let Judea have its own independence. The needs of the empire had to come first.

But there were also those promises of God. He had spoken through the mouth of His prophets that the day would come when a king would rise and His people would be free. We read some of them last week. The hope had grown dim in many souls, and the light of expectation had all but gone out. But there were a few souls—and Simeon was one of them—a faithful remnant who "looked for the consolation of Israel."

How are you at holding on to hope when things look dark? How are you at praying when prayers seem unheard or unanswered? There is an old hymn which comes to mind:

Unanswered yet, the prayer your lips are bringing. . . .

Many of us need, almost more than anything else, to practice our faith as Simeon did. No matter how dark it looked on the outside, inside, in the stronghold of the place of prayer, there was light. And there is always light if we will seek it in the right place. It is not in the latest newscast. It is not in the latest prediction of those who claim to know what is going to happen this year, or next. The light is in the sure promise of God, that no prayer is unheard, and that He will keep His promises.

Luke tells us that Simeon was "inspired by the Spirit" to come to the temple at the particular time when Mary and Joseph had brought the infant Jesus "to do for him according to the custom of the law." (verse 27) These "divine coincidents" happen to us all. We may take them for granted and forget them, or we may see them as little confirmations that we are known and loved, and that God is active in helping us make the right decision at the right time.

As soon as Simeon saw the holy family, he knew what it meant. Jesus was God's fulfillment of His promise. Simeon could now "depart in peace" because he had been allowed to see the salvation of God. His life was now complete.

That term is one to hold onto. "The consolation of Israel." Who is this Jesus? He is just that: the consoler of the broken, one who brings relief from anxiety and trouble.

Prayer: O blessed Lord, when the clouds are dark and foreboding, when the answer to prayer seems too long delayed, and faith grows dim, help me to remember Simeon, and like him, continue to look for and wait for "the consolation of Israel." Thank You for Your faithful relief from stress and anxiety as I turn to You in my need. In Jesus' name. Amen.

1. How is Simeon an example of a Spirit led life?

2. What did God reveal to Simeon about Jesus?

The Witness of John the Baptist

Scripture: John 1:29–37

Text: And John bore witness, "I saw the Spirit descend as a dove from heaven, and it remained on Him." (John 1:32)

John the Baptist already had a following when Jesus appeared at the Jordan River to be baptized. John had grown up, at least part of his life, in the desert area of Judea. There are many speculations about where he lived and how he received his preparation for his prophetic ministry. However it came about, his appearance at that particular time had a dramatic effect on many people high and low. Priests and Levites were sent from Jerusalem to ask, "Who are you?" The religious leaders knew enough about the history of God's dealings with them to recognize that there was, in all probability, a "prophet among them."

John's answer was clear: "I am not the Messiah. I am not the Christ. I am a voice crying in the wilderness. Make straight the way of the Lord." Many heard him and were moved to turn from their sins and renew their faith. "The kingdom of heaven is at hand," John said.

Then Jesus appeared, asking to be baptized. John recognized Him as one who did not need to be baptized, because baptism was a confession of sin and a cleansing from it. "I need to be baptized by You," John said to Jesus. "Let it be this way now," answered Jesus. "It is fitting for me to fulfill all righteousness." (Matthew 3:15) In this way Jesus identified Himself with us all. Baptism was a picture of death and burial. As we sinful, mortal men and women must undergo death and burial, the Lord of life Himself identifies with us. "He was numbered with the transgressors." And Jesus in His baptism also identifies with those who believe and are turning to God. The message of John and the message of Jesus was: "The kingdom of God is at hand; repent and believe the Good News." Jesus was underscoring the truth of John's prophetic message by His baptism.

John was looking for something or someone. He was preaching that the kingdom was "at hand." Some even said that the language could mean "The kingdom of God *is here*." At any rate, things were not going along as they had for generations. A new time had come, and John was looking, watching for some signal that would verify what he had been given inwardly. And God did not disappoint him. When Jesus came, John saw the evidence he needed. This was not just another candidate for baptism. Once the promised sign had been witnessed, John was ready to give his unqualified testimony. "He on whom you see the Spirit descend and remain, this is He who baptizes with the Holy Spirit." (verse 33)

John's testimony is like the opening theme in John's Gospel. Every story and incident in that Gospel are a commentary on the one truth: "I have seen and have borne witness that this is the Son of God." (verse 34) It is significant, too, that he identifies Jesus as the one who baptizes with the Holy Spirit. That is a little-understood ministry of the Lord, but one that continues to this day. He not only comes as Savior and Sin-bearer. He comes as the one who immerses and fills His children with the same Holy Spirit who descended and rested on Him that day at Jordan. It is the gift of love to us all that He brings freely, to enable us to bear fruit to His glory and to bear witness to His love. This is Jesus who loves us, this is the Son of God.

Prayer: Almighty God, as You sent Your well-beloved Son Jesus to be our Savior and Lord, let Your Holy Spirit fill and guide us into all truth. Enable us to delight in Your will and walk in Your ways; to the glory of Your name; through the same Jesus Christ our Lord. Amen.

1. How does John's life exemplify obedience?

2. What does baptism signify?

She Bore Witness to Me

Scripture: John 4:7–18, 27–30

*Text: "Come, see a man who told me all that I ever did.
Can this be the Christ?"* (John 4:29)

Jesus' conversation with the Samaritan woman is one of the most interesting stories in the Gospel. Here was a woman who was going about, minding her own business, as it were, and all of a sudden Jesus appears in her life. He was tired and thirsty and in need of a drink of water. Breaking the custom of the time, he asked her for a drink.

We should stop right there and think about how the Lord subjects Himself to others. It would seem quite in character with a "superman" kind of Savior for Him to cause water to come forth from the earth miraculously, as Moses was allowed to do before the people of Israel. But that was not Jesus' way, and it is still not. He still waits for us to decide, to consent to serve Him. He does not force us. And that tells us a lot about who Jesus is.

This woman was probably a near–outcast in her society. Married five times, she was now living in "open sin" with someone who was not her husband. But Jesus did not despise her for her sinfulness. Instead, He offered her new life, the living water which would spring up and be an ever-flowing well of life. He did not even spend time trying to convince her that she was wrong. He simply let her know who He was, and let her know that who she was was known.

She left her jar at the well and ran to tell others. Her only testimony was that she had met someone who knew all about her. He "told me all that I ever did!" she said. "Could this be the Christ?" That was testimony enough to bring out many to

131

see for themselves. At their invitation, Jesus stayed with them two days, and when Jesus left, they said, "Now we have heard for ourselves, and we know that this is indeed the Savior of the world." (verse 42) Her testimony was a humble one indeed, but it had in it the seed of life.

It is significant, too, that this took place in Samaria, because the Samaritans were considered a lesser breed by the Jews of that time. This is an early indication that Jesus came to bring good news not only to Israel, but to the world. "We know that this is indeed the Savior of the world." In the book of Acts, just before He ascended into heaven, Jesus said to the disciples, "You shall receive power when the Holy Spirit has come upon you; and you shall be my witnesses in Jerusalem and in all Judea and Samaria and to the end of the earth." (Acts 1:8)

The woman's need was her only claim to Jesus' gift. It was all she needed. The same is true for us. It is not our goodness, our achievements, our morality, our "rightness" that makes us dear to God. Our need is our only claim. And it is enough. Our witness, humble as it may be, can also be a means of letting others know that here, indeed, is "the Savior of the world," ready to meet them and give them the living water of life.

Prayer: Thank You, Lord, that we do not have to bring great qualifications to have a living, life-changing relationship with You. Thank You for letting us know that we are known and that we are loved. In Jesus' name. Amen.

1. In what ways did Jesus challenge this woman's understanding of her world?

2. In her conversation with Jesus, what was it that touched the woman most deeply?

The Man Born Blind

Scripture: John 9:1–12, 24–25

Text: Whether he is a sinner, I do not know; one thing I know, that though I was blind, now I see." (John 9:25)

There is not a lot you can do with a miracle. You can acknowledge it, believe it, and give God the glory for it, or—you can choose to disbelieve it and try to explain it away.

The Pharisees were strict observers of the law. To them, following the letter of the law was very, very important. Keeping the Sabbath was one of the primary ways in which they showed their devotion to God. Over and over again Jesus ran into this rigid, legalistic spirit and tried patiently to deal with it. He even reminded them that if one of their animals were in trouble, they would "violate" the Sabbath by trying to save the animal. But His words fell on deaf ears. It did not change their hearts.

The blind beggar had sat waiting for handouts for many a year. He had been born blind. The disciples were like us. They wanted an explanation for why things were the way they were. We all tend to ask such questions: Why is this condition? Why does this child suffer? Who has made this necessary? A well-known pediatric cancer specialist said that she finds that whenever children are diagnosed with cancer, the first question the parents ask is, "What have I done to deserve this?" Jesus is telling us here that there is a mystery in sickness and suffering, and sometimes it is allowed in order that God's glory may be seen and realized through the experience.

When the blind man went as he was told to the pool called Siloam, "he came back seeing." Life would no longer be the same for him. Everything had changed. But he was not allowed to enjoy his new healing. The adversaries of Jesus were still intent on finding reason to accuse Him. And so the newly healed blind man was called before them and questioned a second time. He had but one word of witness. He did not know Jesus, apparently knew very little about Him. But there was that overwhelming evidence every time he opened his eyes. "One thing I know."

His words have been sung by many generations of people, and even now one hears them in an amazing variety of settings:

I once was lost but now am found,
Was blind, but now I see.

There is no greater healing than that of our spiritual blindness. How many stumble and fall in the dark of their own misguided thinking, the blindness of soul. They forget who they are, what they were created for; they forget that they have a loving Father in heaven, and that life is more than they have allowed it to be. And then, by a miracle of grace, their eyes are opened. They begin to love what they hated, and to hate what they loved. They find their hearts tender toward God and filled with concern for others. They find that they can forgive and let go old grudges and resentments. Why? "Though I was blind, now I see." That is what Jesus had done for that blind man, and what He does for blind souls every day.

Prayer: Lord, I thank You for the testimony of this man who was born blind and then given sight. I thank You that You have shed light into the darkness of my soul, and given me new eyes to see the truth. Give me grace to bear a faithful witness. "Was blind, but now I see." Amen.

1. How does our often times rigidity of thinking keep us from experiencing the love and grace of God?

2. For the formerly blind man, what was the bottom line?

The Witness of Pilate

Scripture: John 18:28–40

Text: I find in Him no fault at all. (John 18:38 KJV)

Sometimes the best way to find out what a person is really like is to hear what his enemies say about him. Pilate's witness goes down in history as that of a weak, vacillating Roman official, who was unwilling to take a stand on his own.

You remember how Pilate's wife came out during the proceedings to tell him that she had "suffered many things in a dream" because of Him? "Have nothing to do with this righteous man," she cautioned him. But Pilate was worried. Was he worried about what Rome would say if things got out of hand? Probably. Was he eager to maintain a working relationship with the Jewish leaders? Probably. Did he really think that by washing his hands before them he could remove the blood of his decision to send Jesus out to be crucified? I wonder! Luke tells us that when he found out that Jesus was from Galilee, he sent Him to Herod, who was in Jerusalem at the time. Anything to get out of making a costly decision!

The little conversation Pilate had with Jesus has been scrutinized many times. We get snippets of it from the different Gospels. He was probably curious about this strange prisoner who did not act like the others brought before him. John records the conversation in some detail (18:33–38). The accusation against Jesus was that He claimed to be "king." "Are you the king of the Jews, then?" asked Pilate. "My kingship is not of this world," Jesus answered. "You say that I am a king. For this I was born, and for this I have come into the world: to bear witness to the truth. Everyone who is of the truth hears my voice." You can say that the table has turned at this point. The questioner is being questioned. Pilate's conscience is being addressed. Will he hear and obey the Truth? His only answer, ringing sadly down the centuries, "What *is* truth?" The answer of one who has given up hearing his inmost spirit.

We live in a time when Pilate's question is commonplace. Ours is an age that has embraced "relativity." It has become popular to say "my truth" and "your truth" as if there were two different kinds of "truth," which means no truth at all. Even the churches which once held that Jesus is "the way, the truth, and the life," have sometimes modified their message to mean "the way *for us*," "the truth *for us*," the life *for us*." No wonder that the generation coming after us is confused and looking in all directions for answers to life's searching questions. Pilate's cynical response freed him, in his own mind, to deliver up Jesus to be crucified. He did not like that conversation, and would be glad to be rid of that voice.

But—not until he had made his witness before the accusers! As soon as he said those fatal words, he went out to the Jews again, and told them, "I find in Him no fault at all." And that stands as the final verdict of the judge who condemned Jesus to death. "No crime. No fault at all."

> Ah, holy Jesus, how hast Thou offended,
> That man to judge Thee hath in hate pretended?

One final avenue was open to Pilate: the custom of releasing a prisoner at Passover. Whom would they choose? Jesus perhaps? No, Barabbas! So Pilate had Jesus beaten again, brought Him out, and said, "I am bringing Him out so you will know I find no crime in Him." But Pilate's weakness before those who sought Jesus' death was now apparent. They would have their say. The final word in this sad story is this: "Then he handed Him over to them to be crucified."

Prayer: Lord, forgive my own weakness before those who deride or criticize You. Forgive the cheap peace I sometimes have bought at the price of betrayal. Lord, give me grace to stand with You and for You in every situation. In Jesus' name. Amen.

1. In this passage, how was the law manipulated to subvert the truth?

2. How can we be on the side of truth (verse 27) and so be able to listen to Jesus?

The Centurion at the Cross

Scripture: Mark 15:33–39

*Text: And when the centurion which stood over against him,
saw that He so cried out and gave up the ghost, he said,
Truly this man was the Son of God.*   *(Mark 15:39)*

This incident with the centurion at the cross is recorded by
Matthew, Luke, and Mark—indicating that they all felt it
was an important witness concerning Jesus.

How people die may say a good deal about what is inside.
We all hope that we will be able to face the "last mortal
strife" with the grace to stay true to the Lord. A hymn says:

O make me Thine forever; and should I fainting be,
Lord, let me never, never outlive my love for Thee.

(Attr. to Bernard of Clairvaux)

The centurion had seen many people die, I think. Death
was no stranger to Roman soldiers, and human life was quite
cheap in these outlying provinces of the great Empire. The
point was to keep people under subjection, to have enough
fear of the iron power of Rome that the *Pax Romana*, the
Roman Peace, would be maintained. The cruelty of the soldiers is evident, too, from the Gospel records. Their torment-
ing of Jesus was unnecessary, and the scourging tried men to
the very limits of their human survival. So suffering and death
were no stranger to this professional soldier.

What, then, made the difference in his reaction to this
death? Crucifixion was the cruelest form of execution Rome
practiced. It was a tortuous death. Legend tells us that St. Paul
was beheaded in Rome, while St. Peter was crucified. The difference? Paul was a Roman citizen, and Rome did not crucify
Roman citizens. But Jesus did not have that distinction. To

them, He was a Galilean preacher who was causing an unwelcome stir among a difficult people.

It is easy to get callous when we associate with suffering. It is easy to put a kind of protective layer over our feelings that keep us from feeling the pain we are witnessing. In this way, sometimes we become unfeeling and insensitive to people we love. We may grow impatient with an aging loved one who has become difficult, and fail to sense the confusion, the grief, and the loss of independence with which he or she is grappling. Friends who work in nursing homes tell me that it is evident that relatives do protect themselves from the pain their loved one is experiencing. Perhaps this had happened to some of these soldiers, which made them cruel rather than humane.

But this centurion had enough vulnerability left in him to be moved by what was happening. First, there was this troublesome inscription at the top of the cross, written in Hebrew, Greek, and Latin. Pilate had insisted on it. JESUS OF NAZARETH, KING OF THE JEWS. A brief conversation had taken place between Jesus and one of the thieves being crucified alongside Him. "Jesus, Lord, remember me when Thou comest into Thy kingdom." The answer came, "Verily I say unto thee, Today shalt thou be with Me in paradise." (Luke 23:42, 43) Had the centurion heard it? I believe so.

And then the sun went out. Darkness covered the earth. It was frightening, and even brave hearts trembled. Then Jesus cried, "Father, into thy hands I commend my spirit." And that was enough for this centurion. "Certainly this was a righteous man." (Luke 23:47) "Truly this man was the Son of God." (Mark 15:39). This is the Jesus, who loves you with eternal love.

Prayer: Lord Jesus, with the centurion I would say, "You are the Son of God." May I love You, worship and adore You with all my heart, mind, soul, and strength, for Your love's sake. Amen.

1. How did Jesus' manner of dying bring authenticity to the designation "King of the Jews"?

2. How can we keep from becoming callous when we are around those who are suffering?

The Witness of Mary Magdalene

Scripture: John 20:1–18

Text: Mary Magdalene went and said to the disciples, "I have seen the Lord"; and she told them that He had said these things to her.
(John 20:18)

Mary had been so filled with grief and confusion that she did not at first recognize the Lord in the garden outside the tomb. She and her friends had run to the tomb early that Sunday morning, "while it was still dark," to finish up their preparation of the body of Jesus for burial. He had been taken down from the cross so late on Friday that there was not time to finish the burial anointing. It was the last thing they could do for their dead leader.

Mary had good reason to linger here. It was this Man who had seen her in her lost and shameful state, had forgiven her sins and pointed her in a new direction. Mary had lived the life of sin and shame, and through the presence of Jesus in her life had found a new hope and a new sense of worth. His love had reached her and had enabled her to live anew.

It is no wonder that Mary Magdalene became a favorite saint of many a soul through the centuries that followed. Many churches bear her name, and always it is a sign of hope for anyone who learns the story of how Mary, the woman who sold herself to others, became Mary, the woman who gave herself wholly to God. There is a wonderful little account in Luke 7 about a visit of Jesus to the home of a Pharisee. The Pharisees were a religious and upright group, careful about keeping themselves right. While they were at supper, "a woman of the city, who was a sinner" came in with an alabaster flask of ointment. She washed Jesus' feet with her tears, kissed them, and anointed them with the ointment. The Pharisee was indignant. He said to himself, "If this man were a prophet, he would have known who and what sort of woman this is who is touching him, for she is a sinner." Ah, Simon! but He did know. And He knows every sinner who comes with tears to His feet and seeks the cleansing of heart He can give. He accepts the act of love which the sinful, cleansed heart pours out on Him, not because it is perfect, but because He sees the heart's condition. To Simon He said, "You gave me not a kiss . . . you did not anoint my head with oil . . . I tell you, he who is forgiven little, loves little." Simon did not know how much he needed to be forgiven. The poor woman did, and she went away with those words ringing in her ears, "Your sins are forgiven."

Now Mary wept as she stood by the tomb of the crucified One, wondering what had happened to His body. Then the "impossible" happened. He called her by name, "Mary!" And suddenly she saw, and knew. He was not dead, but alive. And He still lives, standing beside us at our tombs, the graves of those we love, the sad and sorrowful times of our lives, calling us by name. Mary saw, and no one could take that from her. In the time that followed, she would remember that He who loved her still lived.

Sad Mary, dry thine eyes, And cease thy woeful cries;
It is no gardener, but thy Lord Who brings thee glad surprise.

(H. C. Robbins)

Prayer: Lord Jesus, You did not turn away from Mary when she came to You, broken and soiled by the world. You do not turn us away when we turn to You in our need, but You accept us, love us, and set us anew on the road of hope and life. For this, most blessed Jesus, accept our thanks and praise. Amen.

1. How had Jesus demonstrated His love to Mary Madgalene?

2. How does the knowledge of God's forgiveness release your heart to love him?

Week Eight

Believe in Me

Believe in Me
The Words, Works, and Actions of the Lord

After the healing of the man born blind, Jesus' opponents decided to stone Him. He had said things that they felt insulted them and brought their own religious commitment into question. There follows in the tenth chapter of John's Gospel an interesting conversation that gives us a clue as to how Jesus felt about His own works and ministries.

The Jews took up stones again to stone Him. Jesus said, "I have shown you many good works from the Father; for which of these do you stone Me?" The Jews answered, "We stone You for no good work but for blasphemy; because You, being a man, make Yourself God." Jesus answered them, . . . "If I am not doing the works of my Father, then do not believe Me; but if I do them, even though you do not believe Me, believe the works, that you may know and understand that the Father is in Me and I am in the Father." (John 10:31-38, selections)

This week, as we finish our eight-week course of study and meditation, we will look at some of these works, words, and actions of the Lord, to see what they tell us about Him.

It is important that we remember that His works point to "who He is." It is so important to *believe* that much, much emphasis is placed on it. Believing opens us up to new life.

Believing casts out the darkness of fear and guilt. Believing allows the sunshine of God's love to penetrate the dark places of our souls. No wonder that He says, "Believe in Me."

Water into Wine

Scripture: John 2:1-11

Text: "But you have kept the good wine until now."
(John 2:10)

John says that the first sign that Jesus did was in Cana of Galilee, *manifesting* His glory to His disciples. We have to read through the four Gospels to get the story of how those twelve men were chosen to be His disciples, and how they responded to the challenge. What was it that caused them to leave their nets and their boats, their tax tables and their other trades to follow this untrained traveling teacher? Only little by little did they come to understand who He was, and even to the end they did not have the complete picture. How like us! It seems to take most of us a very long time and many, many experiences to *begin* to appreciate and appropriate the wonder of the love which has found us and claimed us.

This is a favorite story of many, because it is one of the few glimpses we have of Jesus' relationship with His mother. Other glimpses show her concern for His welfare and her presence on some of His journeys, along with other women who supported and cared for the band of disciples. But this is a strictly social occasion, or so it seems. "A marriage at Cana in Galilee, and the mother of Jesus was there. Jesus was also *invited* to the marriage."

Marriages in that area were the largest and most festive social occasions people ever knew. They still are. This writer was with a choir in Czechoslovakia in 1989. We stopped to see a certain historic building, where, as it happened, a wedding reception was going on—photographs, etc. To our great surprise, the hosts of the wedding celebration insisted that we

147

all taste the special plum wine or brandy which they were using to toast the bride and groom. So there we were, forty-five complete strangers, invited to the wedding celebration.

Jesus was at home in time of joy and in time of sorrow. It is important that we invite Him to our homes and hearts in both cases. Times of joy can be times of forgetting, times of indulging. They can be dangerous times. Times of sorrow can be times of self-pity and bitterness. In both cases, Jesus' presence can make all the difference.

Jesus' mother said an important word that has rung in Christian hearts down through the centuries. When she had informed Jesus of the need, she simply said to the servants, "Do whatever He tells you." She could leave it at that. There can be no better counsel then or now. "Do whatever He tells you," and wonderful things will happen.

The normal celebration had run dry. They often do. We may try to make ourselves feel good in many ways, but sooner or later, our techniques run dry. "When the wine failed. . . ." Our earthly joys always fail, and then we have the opportunity to experience a miracle too great for words. In that failure, in that need, a new wine comes. Something unexpected and unexplainable enters the picture. The steward could not understand or explain it, so he called the bridegroom for an explanation. "Most people would serve the best first, and then the poorer quality; but you have kept the good wine until now." That is still God's way.

Prayer: O Lord our God, You are the Author and Giver of all good things. Turning from our little pleasures and failing fantasies, may we taste the new wine of Your grace, and be filled with Your joy; through Jesus Christ our Lord. Amen.

1. What was the fruit or outcome of Jesus' first miracle?

2. How is an understanding of God's love being built in your life?

Power Has Gone Forth from Me

Scripture: Luke 8:42b-48

*Text: "Someone touched me, for I perceive that power
has gone forth from Me."   (Luke 8:46)*

There are two kinds of touches. There is the touch that
gives blessing and strength. There is the touch that draws
blessing and strength from another. Both kinds have their
place and fulfill a need.

There have been times in the life of this writer when my
wife's presence and touch were very important in getting
through a hard time. It is easy to feel ashamed of such need and
weakness, but in the moment of need, shame is overcome and
one reaches out for reassurance. It is a form of spiritual pride,
I think, to suppose that we are so strong, so independent, so
"spiritual" that we do not need the help of another human
being. I can remember, too, as a child, when my mother's hand
on my forehead seemed to bring a reassurance that all would
be all right. That loving, blessing touch is a universal need.

The church has recognized that in the "laying on of
hands." In the book of James the writer says, "Is any sick
among you? Let them call for the elders of the church, and let
them pray over him, *anointing* him with oil in the name of the
Lord; and the prayer of faith will save the sick man, and the
Lord will raise him up." (James 5:14,15a) It is not just the oil,
but the act of anointing, of touching that brings the blessing.
In this case, the elders are performing the act "in the place of
Christ," that is, in the name of Christ and as extensions of the
divine touch.

But what about that other touch? The woman whose sickness had extended over eighteen long years had heard of Jesus

and believed in her heart that if she could just touch His garment, that would be enough. And so she determinedly made her way through the crowd on her mission of need. At last she was near enough, and trembling, she stretched forth her hand, probably hoping that no one would notice. The curious conversation that took place then tells us a lot about the Lord. "Who touched me?" Jesus asked. The disciples were amazed. The crowd was pressing in one every side, jostling, pushing. "Master, the multitudes surround You and press upon You!" But Jesus would not be put off. Someone in need had stretched forth the hand of faith, and He wanted to speak to that person. "Someone touched me; for I perceive that power has gone forth from me." How frightened the poor woman was, then, to be found out! But, no. It was not anger, but mercy and encouragement that she saw in His face. "Daughter, your faith has made you well! Go in peace!" She would never have to feel guilty about what she had done.

Faith makes a claim on Jesus that He cannot deny. That's a bold statement, but one that I believe is true. Faith makes a claim on our heavenly Father that He cannot, will not turn away. It is His delight that we believe in Him enough to press our way through the crowds of conflict, the thickets of doubt, and stretch forth the trembling hand to touch His garment, *believing* that our faith is not in vain! What does *that* tell you about this Jesus who loves you?

Prayer: Lord, give me such a faith as pressed that poor woman to touch Your garment's hem. There may I find all I need for every need. I ask it for Your name's sake. Amen.

1. What can give us the boldness to "touch the hem of his garment?"

2. In what area of your life do you need the healing power of Jesus?

The Centurion and His Servant

Scripture: Luke 7:1-10

Text: "I tell you not even in Israel have I found such faith."
(Luke 7:9)

We get some idea of who Jesus is by His relationship with people who were not Jews. There was the Syro-Phoenecian woman, the woman by the well in Samaria, and this centurion and his servant. It is clear that He cared for people regardless of race or background.

This centurion at Capernaum is a special case in point. They still show to tourists and pilgrims the ruins of the synagogue which he helped to build. In this story we see that some of the soldiers who were stationed to keep the Jewish nation in subjugation to Rome were affected by the obvious superiority of Jewish worship over that which they had witnessed in other religions. Here was a people who worshipped an invisible God who would allow no graven images. There were no fertility rites or other immoral displays under the guise of religion, but a stress on purity and holiness before God. And this man was moved by it. He had become a believer in the God of Israel.

When one got sick in those days, there were no hospitals, and very few physicians available. Probably in an out-of-the-way place like Capernaum there were none at all. This explains why there was such an eager following after anyone who showed signs of healing gifts. This is the background of the centurion's request. But there is something more in this story. There was a humility and respect shown toward Jesus that He had not experienced among His own countrymen. At that time the home of a Gentile was considered unsuitable for a Jew to enter. This is probably the reason the centurion sent word to

Jesus not to "trouble Yourself, for I am not worthy to have You come under my roof." Can we really appreciate Jesus' worthiness without appreciating our own unworthiness? The hymn says, "Two wonders I confess: the wonder of His matchless love, and my unworthiness." The centurion had that wonderful gift of knowing his unfitness. That is the knowledge that brings us to confession, repentance, and forgiveness. Without it, we remain, like the Pharisee, caught up in our rightness and worth.

And there is still more. The centurion has such faith in Jesus that he compares it to his own power over the soldiers under him. A centurion was commander of a hundred men. He uses the comparison of his authority to express his unqualified belief that Jesus has power and authority over the sickness and condition of his servant. That is what made Jesus exclaim, "I tell you, not even in Israel have I found such faith!"

As the Lord moves in and out of people's lives, going about "doing good," as the Gospel says, He calls for hearts to believe the good news. God is alive. God cares. The rule and kingdom of God have drawn near. We can enter that world and live in it, *if we believe and choose to do so*. That is what He wants for us. That is what He makes possible for us— centurion (ruler) and servant (slave) alike. It makes no difference to Him who we are. His love knows no bounds, and it is for us. His will for us is life. And that life comes in response to our choice of faith.

Prayer: Lord, I confess that I often hold back the blessing You would give through my lack of trust and faith. I am sorry for this, and I choose to believe in Your goodness and Your good will. Help my unbelief! In Jesus' name. Amen.

1. What was unusual about the character of the centurion?

2. How can one reconcile his humility with his authority?

Feeding the Five Thousand

Scripture: Matthew 14:13-21

Text: And they all ate and were satisfied. And they took up twelve baskets full of the broken pieces left over.   (Matthew 14:20)

That is the way it is with God. When we receive what He has to give us, we will be ultimately satisfied. In Isaiah 55:2, God asks, "Why do you spend your money for that which is not bread, and your labor for that which does not satisfy?" Why indeed! Yet we have all done this, seeking satisfaction where there is none. The Israelites had bread from heaven, but became bored with it and lusted after flesh. They found to their sorrow that what they craved brought not satisfaction, but sorrow and death.

The people who had followed Jesus out into the desert place were seeking Bread for the soul. They did not fully understand His message, but something in it drew them and they wanted to hear more. They saw the works He did, and they believed that He was sent from God. In that eagerness they stayed beyond the provisions they had made for their journey. Their need became the opportunity for God's power to be shown in a new situation. Again, let it remind us that every new situation, every new need is an opportunity for God's power to be displayed in your life and mine. We need the eyes of faith to see, but the power is there, sufficient for it, whatever it may be.

We take for granted that a little seed can be sown into the ground and then produce a large plant with abundant fruit and many more seeds. We call the process natural, but is it not another demonstration of God's power to multiply and increase beyond any real explanation? Who understands the process by which a mustard seed becomes a large plant in which the birds of the air can sit? Oh, for eyes to see His power at work in everyday life!

I love that phrase in Matthew's Gospel, after the people had been fed and satisfied: "Twelve baskets full left over." Not only divine increase according to need, but a divine overflow. God blesses us in our need, but the blessing does not stop with us. It overflows to others. In that sense no blessing is private. It always has in it the capacity to overflow to bless others. When we allow God to begin to change us, for example, it will inevitably overflow to others whose lives are closely connected with ours. It will become a channel of blessing to them as we allow Him to deal with us in our need. And that is the way He works with all His children.

It is important to see the motivation for this great miracle—one so significant that it is included in every Gospel. "As He went ashore, He saw a great throng; and He had compassion on them and healed their sick." (verse 14) Here it is again: their need drew His compassionate heart. How foolish we are then, to try to hide our need and make it alone! "O what peace we often forfeit, O what needless pain we bear, all because we do not carry everything to God in prayer."

Prayer: For all the times You have multiplied blessings to meet our needs, and for the marvelous overflow of Your blessing in my life, I thank and praise You, Lord Jesus Christ! Amen.

1. Why had Jesus withdrawn to this solitary place?

2. In light of this, what does his response to the crowds tell us about him? (vs.14)

Let the Children Come to Me

Scripture: Mark 10:13-16

*Text: Let the children come to Me, do not hinder them;
for to such belongs the kingdom of God.   (Mark 10:14)*

"Out of the mouths of babes and sucklings Thou hast ordained strength." "A little child shall lead them." "Let the children come to me, do not hinder them."

When the mothers in this Gospel incident heard Jesus speak about God and the plan of God for His creation, they wanted their children to know more of Him. They wanted Him to convey some blessing on them. They had seen or heard how He laid hands on sick people and they became well. They had seen or heard how He touched troubled people and they became whole again. And they wanted this for their children.

We all want the best for our children, but we do not always know what is best. Sometimes, in our desire to have them love us and not be angry at us, we allow them to do things that are hurtful, even harmful for their souls. Is this not the case in many families today, with relaxed supervision and relaxed standards for our young? Yet the yearning in all of us who have children, young or old, is for their best.

Jesus tells us a lot about Himself and about the nature of His rule in this little Gospel story. He says that the kingdom of God belongs to the childlike. I don't believe that He romanticized childhood and thought that children were all good. Rather, I think He was extolling that quality of openness, the receptivity that childhood has before it becomes jaded with too much knowledge and thinks it knows best.

It was this writer's privilege years ago to be a leader in a church camp of fourth and fifth graders. The boys were full of questions, and were quite ready to listen to answers. They were enthusiastic about exploring the woods and lake, and were even afraid of the dark at night. And so they were a joy to be with for those ten strenuous days. The child-like spirit had not been outgrown. Alas when it is! Alas when we begin to think that we know more than the adults. Alas when we think that ours is the first generation that really understands, and looks down on the wisdom and experience of former generations! We are most surely missing the kingdom in that case.

What do we learn from the little child who so willingly believes in God, who so willingly believes that Jesus loves him or her? We learn that we can set aside our grown-up distortions and become open to wonder again. We can let the hard crust of cynicism be broken and learn to expect that the goodness of God is greater than the pains and difficulties of life. It is a matter of choice.

The Lord still calls us "children." We are *His* children, and His love reaches out to us. Were we brought to Him as little children through the faith of parents? Most of us were. But however you found your way to Him, He owns you as His own, and calls you to come "as a little child" to Him in every need.

Prayer: Lord Jesus, You took the children in Your arms and blessed them. May we know that same touch on our lives today as we wait for Your blessing; for Your love's sake. Amen.

1. In this passage, compare the attitude of the people, the disciples, and Jesus.

2. How did Jesus communicate his love for the children?

My House is a House of Prayer

Scripture: Mark 11:15-19

Text: Is it not written, "My house is a house of prayer for all the nations"? (Mark 11:17)

When Jesus saw the multitudes scattered as sheep without a shepherd, His heart was "moved with compassion" toward them. When He entered Jerusalem and considered how she had treated the prophets that were sent to her, and what awaited Him in the holy city, "he wept over it." But there are few incidents in the Gospels that show Jesus' anger or indignation. One was when the children were being brought to Him and the disciples turned them away. Another was when He went into the temple and saw the traffic in trade that flourished there.

The temple was important to the life of God's people. It was the great unifying symbol which spoke of their special relation to God. Jesus' parents took Him to the temple when He was ready to be circumcised, and when He was twelve, He stayed back asking questions of the doctors. When His mother found Him after three days of searching, He asked, "Did you not know that I must be in my Father's house?" (Luke 2:40) Jesus had His disciples watch as people came and put their money into the temple treasury. There they watched a widow who put in two little coins—"all her living"—and Jesus commended her to them for what she had done. The temple was not only important to the life of God's people. It was important to Jesus Himself.

As He taught in the temple, He compared it to His own body, saying, "Tear this temple down and I will raise it up in three days." But His enemies used those words against Him, and accused Him of saying *He* would tear down the temple and raise it up in three days. Whenever He came to Jerusalem, it seems that He made His way into the temple and taught the people there.

This time He was moved beyond mere words. "The zeal of Thy house hath eaten me up," John's Gospel quotes later from the Psalmist. There is no mistaking here that God's wrath as well as His mercy is an active part of His nature. Anyone who cannot be indignant in the face of great wrong cannot be trusted to support what is good. We need to think about that when we confront the evils of our day. Too many people try to maintain a neutral stance when integrity would call forth an indignation like Jesus shows here. I would not want a Savior who was indifferent to human cruelty and evil. The book of Revelation pictures under the altar of heaven the souls of those who have been slain for the word of God, for the witness they have made. Their continual cry is, "O Sovereign Lord, holy and true, how long before Thou wilt judge and avenge our blood on those who dwell upon the earth?" (Rev. 6:10) Billy Graham said, when he spoke in the Rotunda of the Capitol in Washington on the occasion of receiving the Congressional Medal of Honor, "Our century has witnessed the outer limits of human evil." Surely the Lord's heart must be moved both to indignation and grief as He beholds the condition of our time.

Jesus cares. And because He cares, He acts. His act in driving out the money-changers show that He still inhabits the House of Prayer, and wants it to remain true to its purpose.

Prayer: Help us to remember, O Lord, that Your indignation against evil is a purifying, saving anger. May we be afraid to offend You more than we are afraid to lose the favor of this world, and find grace to meet You faithfully in the place of prayer. In Jesus' name. Amen.

1. As well as disrupting the trade in the temple, what else did Jesus do? (vs. 17)

2. Why did the priests and teachers want to kill Jesus?

The Raising of Lazarus

Scripture: John 11:1-15

Text: Lazarus is dead; and for your sake I am glad I was not there, so that you may believe.   (John 11:15)

Of all the miracles recorded in the Gospels, the raising of Lazarus is perhaps the most dramatic and mind-boggling. Not only was Lazarus dead, but by the time Jesus and the disciples arrived back at Bethany, he had been dead four days.

What are we to make of this? There is nothing that produces more fear and deep anxiety in the human heart than the knowledge that we are mortal. Death, as the Bible tells us, is the final enemy to be overcome. The Book of Hebrews says, "Since therefore the children share in flesh and blood, He Himself likewise partook of the same nature, that through death He might destroy him who has the power of death, that is, the devil, and deliver all those who through fear of death were subject to lifelong bondage." (Hebrews 2:14, 15) So when Jesus meets death in His friend Lazarus, and calls forth Lazarus out of death, He is saying something very, very important to all of us who still in any measure live "in fear of death" and its bondage.

How kind of God to design a miracle like this "so that you might believe"! We hear all kinds of explanations of "near-death experiences," and our modern, scientific, materialistic minds look for explanations that rule out the miraculous. Yet we are surrounded by miracles every day without realizing it or recognizing them. Every believer can surely say that his or her life is "a miracle" when we realize how many "dangers, toils, and snares" we have already come through. When we see God's protecting hand over us and our loved ones, we can surely bow our heads before the God who raises the dead!

And that's exactly what this miracle of the raising of Lazarus says to you and me. There are no extremities beyond which God cannot go. There are no limits to what He can do, except that which His own nature imposes on Him. He cannot lie. He cannot prove false to Himself. He cannot be other than what He is. But death holds no power over Him. Jesus proved that at the grave of Lazarus, and the high priest's crowd was too blind to see it. Instead of bowing in awe before this demonstration of divine power, they plotted all the more how to rid themselves of Jesus.

If we are honest with ourselves, most of us will have to admit that we still have lingering fears connected with death. It seems to threaten to undo us, to blot us out, to remove us from existence. It always carries with it the devil's lie that he holds the trump card in the game of life. Many people look at death as an unmitigated tragedy, the sad conclusion of the story. Even many Christians fail at this point to go all the way to Lazarus' tomb with Mary and Martha. Both those sisters said, "Lord, if you had been here, my brother would not have died." But Martha went even further. She added to that, "Even now I know that whatever you ask from God, God will give you." (verse 22)

Today's look at Jesus, going with His friends to the tomb of His friend Lazarus is meant to reassure us that to any place we are called to go, including the tomb, He will go with us. This is the Jesus who loves us.

Prayer: Abide with us, O Lord, and go with us as we walk this pilgrim way. We believe in You, and want to grow more steady in our faith and faithfulness. In Jesus' name. Amen.

1. Humanly speaking, what would be the reasons for Jesus to go or not to go to Bethany?

2. Jesus uses metaphors pertaining to day and night, sleeping and waking. To what did they refer?